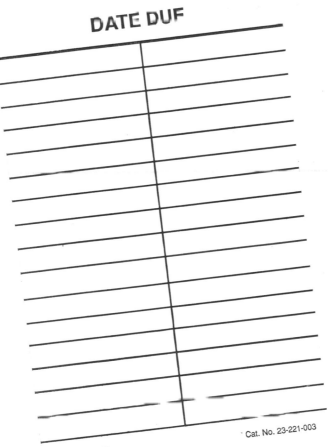

DATE DUE

Cat. No. 23-221-003

BRODART, CO.

Bloom's Modern Critical Views

African American Poets:
Wheatley-Tolson
Edward Albee
American and Canadian
Women Poets,
1970–present
American Women
Poets, 1650–1950
Maya Angelou
Asian-American Writers
Margaret Atwood
Jane Austen
James Baldwin
Honoré de Balzac
Samuel Beckett
Saul Bellow
The Bible
William Blake
Jorge Luis Borges
Ray Bradbury
The Brontës
Gwendolyn Brooks
Elizabeth Barrett
Browning
Robert Browning
Italo Calvino
Albert Camus
Lewis Carroll
Willa Cather
Cervantes
Geoffrey Chaucer
Anton Chekhov
Kate Chopin
Agatha Christie
Samuel Taylor
Coleridge
Joseph Conrad
Contemporary Poets
Stephen Crane
Dante
Daniel Defoe
Don DeLillo
Charles Dickens
Emily Dickinson
John Donne and the
17th-Century Poets
Fyodor Dostoevsky
W.E.B. Du Bois

George Eliot
T. S. Eliot
Ralph Ellison
Ralph Waldo Emerson
William Faulkner
F. Scott Fitzgerald
Sigmund Freud
Robert Frost
Johan Wolfgang von
Goethe
George Gordon, Lord
Byron
Graham Greene
Thomas Hardy
Nathaniel Hawthorne
Ernest Hemingway
Hispanic-American
Writers
Homer
Langston Hughes
Zora Neale Hurston
Aldous Huxley
Henrik Ibsen
John Irving
Henry James
James Joyce
Franz Kafka
John Keats
Jamaica Kincaid
Stephen King
Rudyard Kipling
Milan Kundera
D. H. Lawrence
Ursula K. Le Guin
Sinclair Lewis
Bernard Malamud
Christopher Marlowe
Gabriel García Márquez
Cormac McCarthy
Carson McCullers
Herman Melville
Arthur Miller
John Milton
Molière
Toni Morrison
Native-American
Writers
Joyce Carol Oates

Flannery O'Connor
Eugene O'Neill
George Orwell
Octavio Paz
Sylvia Plath
Edgar Allan Poe
Katherine Anne Porter
J. D. Salinger
Jean-Paul Sartre
William Shakespeare:
Histories and Poems
William Shakespeare:
Romances
William Shakespeare:
The Comedies
William Shakespeare:
The Tragedies
George Bernard Shaw
Mary Wollstonecraft
Shelley
Percy Bysshe Shelley
Alexander
Solzhenitsyn
Sophocles
John Steinbeck
Tom Stoppard
Jonathan Swift
Amy Tan
Alfred, Lord Tennyson
Henry David Thoreau
J. R. R. Tolkien
Leo Tolstoy
Mark Twain
John Updike
Kurt Vonnegut
Alice Walker
Robert Penn Warren
Eudora Welty
Edith Wharton
Walt Whitman
Oscar Wilde
Tennessee Williams
Thomas Wolfe
Tom Wolfe
Virginia Woolf
William Wordsworth
Richard Wright
William Butler Yeats

Modern Critical Views

CARSON McCULLERS

Edited and with an introduction by
Harold Bloom
Sterling Professor of the Humanities
Yale University

CHELSEA HOUSE PUBLISHERS
Philadelphia

Jacket illustration by Sante Graziani

Carson McCullers is seen against the background of a crucial scene in her Reflections in a Golden Eye, *as the desperately love-sick soldier stations himself at the bedside of his beloved. She knows neither of his vigil nor of his passion.* —H.B.

© 1986 by Chelsea House Publishers,
a subsidiary of Haights Cross Communications

Introduction © 1986 by Harold Bloom

Printed and bound in the United States of America

10   9   8

∞ The paper used in this publication meets the minimum requirements of the American National Standard for Permanence of Paper for Printed Library Materials, Z39.48-1984.

Library of Congress Cataloging-in-Publication Data
Carson McCullers.
    (Modern critical views)
    Bibliography: p.
    Includes index.
    1. McCullers, Carson, 1917–1967—Criticism and interpretation.   I. Bloom, Harold.   II. Series.
PS3525.A1772Z584   1986   813'.52   86-9718
ISBN 0-87754-630-4

Contents

Editor's Note

This book brings together a representative selection of the best criticism yet published upon the fiction of Carson McCullers, arranged in the chronological order of its original publication. I am grateful to Susan Laity, Henry Finder, and Caroline Rebecca Rogers for their aid in editing this volume.

My introduction centers upon *The Heart Is a Lonely Hunter* and *The Ballad of the Sad Café*, emphasizing McCullers's curious strength in representing a universal hunger for love, however grotesquely that hunger manifests itself. Marguerite Young begins the chronological sequence of criticism with an appreciation of *The Member of the Wedding*, which is followed here by the enthusiastic tribute to *Reflections in a Golden Eye* by Tennessee Williams, and by Gore Vidal's genial but more reserved appraisal of *Clock Without Hands*.

Oliver Evans expounds the allegory of McCullers's drama *The Square Root of Wonderful*, while Klaus Lubbers provides a full-scale overview of McCullers's entire achievement. The three early novels—*Heart, Reflections, Ballad*—are unified in the analysis of Lawrence Graver, while Richard M. Cook devotes himself wholly to the problematic and disturbing *Reflections*. Another general estimate, but centered upon the *Ballad*, is given by Richard Gray, a learned student of southern American literature.

More recent criticism, reflecting the perspectives of the 1980s, begins here with Margaret B. McDowell's exegesis of the short stories and the poems, and continues with Louise Westling's and Mary Ann Dazey's reconsiderations of what may be McCullers's masterpiece, *The Ballad of the Sad Café*. A final analysis, Barbara A. White's account of *The Member of the Wedding*, provides a fresh illumination upon the fate of the erotic self in McCullers, and seems to me a hopeful portent of directions in which the future criticism of McCullers's fiction may choose to move.

Introduction

I

"I become the characters I write about and I bless the Latin poet Terence who said 'Nothing human is alien to me.'" That was the aesthetic credo of Carson McCullers, and was her program for a limited yet astonishingly intense art of fiction. Rereading her after nearly twenty years away from her novels and stories, I discover that time has enhanced *The Heart Is a Lonely Hunter* and *The Ballad of the Sad Café*, and perhaps rendered less problematic *Reflections in a Golden Eye*. What time cannot do is alter the burden for critics that McCullers represents. Her fiction, like her person, risked that perpetual crisis of Eros of which D. H. Lawrence was the poet and Freud the theoretician. Call it the tendency to make false connections, as set forth by Freud with mordant accuracy in the second paragraph of his crucial paper of 1912, "The Dynamics of the Transference":

> Let us bear clearly in mind that every human being has acquired, by the combined operation of inherent disposition and of external influences in childhood, a special individuality in the exercise of his capacity to love—that is, in the conditions which he sets up for loving, in the impulses he gratifies by it, and in the aims he sets out to achieve in it. This forms a *cliché* or stereotype in him, so to speak (or even several), which perpetually repeats and reproduces itself as life goes on, in so far as external circumstances and the nature of the accessible love-objects permit, and is indeed itself to some extent modifiable by later impressions. Now our experience has shown that of these feelings which determine the capacity to love only a part has undergone full psychical development; this part is directed towards reality, and can be made use of by the conscious personality, of which it forms part. The other part of these libidinal impulses has been held up in development, withheld from the conscious personality and from reality, and may either expend itself only in phantasy, or may

1

remain completely buried in the unconscious so that the conscious personality is unaware of its existence. Expectant libidinal impulses will inevitably be roused, in anyone whose need for love is not being satisfactorily gratified in reality, by each new person coming upon the scene, and it is more than probable that both parts of the libido, the conscious and the unconscious, will participate in this attitude.

All of McCullers's characters share a particular quirk in the exercise of their capacity to love—they exist, and eventually expire, by falling in love with a hopeless hope. Their authentic literary ancestor is Wordsworth's poignant Margaret, in *The Ruined Cottage*, and like his Margaret they are destroyed, not by despair, but by the extravagance of erotic hope. It is no accident that McCullers's first and best book should bear, as title, her most impressive, indeed unforgettable metaphor: *The Heart Is a Lonely Hunter*.

McCullers's few ventures into literary criticism, whether of Gogol, Faulkner, or herself, were not very illuminating, except in their obsession with loneliness. Her notes on writing, "The Flowering Dream," record her violent, physical response to reading Anne Frank's diary, which caused a rash to break out on her hands and feet. The fear of insulation clearly was the enabling power of McCullers's imagination. When she cited Faulkner and Eugene O'Neill as her major influences, she surprisingly added the Flaubert of *Madame Bovary*, where we might have expected the Lawrence of *The Rainbow* and "The Prussian Officer." But it was Emma's *situation* rather than Flaubert's stance or style that engrossed her.

Mick Kelly, McCullers's surrogate in *The Heart Is a Lonely Hunter*, remains her absolute achievement at representing a personality, presumably a vision of her own personality at the age of twelve. Vivid as the other lonely hunters are— the deaf mute John Singer; Biff Brannon, the café proprietor; Jake Blount, alcoholic revolutionary; Dr. Benedict Mady Copeland, black liberal and reformer— the book still lives in the tormented intensity of Mick Kelly, who knows early to be "grieved to think how power and will / In opposition rule our mortal day, / And why God made irreconcilable / Good and the means of Good." That is the dark wisdom of Shelley in *The Triumph of Life*, but it is also a wisdom realized perfectly and independently by Mick Kelly, who rightly fears the triumph of life over her own integrity, her own hope, her own sense of potential for achievement or for love. The Shelleyan passage becomes pure McCullers if we transpose it to: "And why God made irreconcilable / Love and the means of Love."

II

The Heart Is a Lonely Hunter would not maintain its force if its only final vision were to be the triumph of life, in Shelley's ironic sense. McCullers gives us a tough-grained, last sense of Mick Kelly, bereaved, thrown back into an absolute loneliness, but ongoing nevertheless:

But now no music was in her mind. That was a funny thing. It was like she was shut out from the inside room. Sometimes a quick little tune would come and go—but she never went into the inside room with music like she used to do. It was like she was too tense. Or maybe because it was like the store took all her energy and time. Woolworth's wasn't the same as school. When she used to come home from school she felt good and was ready to start working on the music. But now she was always tired. At home she just ate supper and slept and then ate breakfast and went off to the store again. A song she had started in her private notebook two months before was still not finished. And she wanted to stay in the inside room but she didn't know how. It was like the inside room was locked somewhere away from her. A very hard thing to understand.

Mick pushed her broken front tooth with her thumb. But she did have Mister Singer's radio. All the installments hadn't been paid and she took on the responsibility. It was good to have something that had belonged to him. And maybe one of these days she might be able to set aside a little for a second-hand piano. Say two bucks a week. And she wouldn't let anybody touch this private piano but her—only she might teach George little pieces. She would keep it in the back room and play on it every night. And all day Sunday. But then suppose some week she couldn't make a payment. So then would they come to take it away like the little red bicycle? And suppose like she wouldn't let them. Suppose she hid the piano under the house. Or else she would meet them at the front door. And fight. She would knock down both the two men so they would have shiners and broke noses and would be passed out on the hall floor.

Mick frowned and rubbed her fist hard across her forehead. That was the way things were. It was like she was mad all the time. Not how a kid gets mad quick so that soon it is all over—but in another way. Only there was nothing to be mad at. Unless the store. But the store hadn't asked her to take the job. So there was nothing to be mad at. It was like she was cheated. Only nobody had cheated her. So there was nobody to take it out on. However, just the same she had that feeling. Cheated.

But maybe it would be true about the piano and turn out O.K. Maybe she would get a chance soon. Else what the hell good had it all been—the way she felt about music and the plans she had made

in the inside room? It had to be some good if anything made sense.
And it was too and it was too and it was too and it was too. It was
some good.

All right!

O.K!

Some good.

One can call this "Portrait of the Artist as a Young Girl," and see Mick as
a visionary of "the way things were." She has the strength of McCullers's endings
that are not wholly negations:

Biff wet his handkerchief beneath the water tap and patted his drawn,
tense face. Somehow he remembered that the awning had not yet
been raised. As he went to the door his walk gained steadiness. And
when at last he was inside again he composed himself soberly to
await the morning sun.

(*The Heart Is a Lonely Hunter*)

Even in death the body of the soldier still had the look of warm,
animal comfort. His grave face was unchanged, and his sun-browned
hands lay palm upwards on the carpet as though in sleep.

(*Reflections in a Golden Eye*)

The most remarkable of these conclusions is the vignette called "The Twelve
Mortal Men" that serves as epilogue or coda to *The Ballad of the Sad Café*:

THE TWELVE MORTAL MEN

The Forks Falls highway is three miles from the town, and it is here
the chain gang has been working. The road is of macadam, and
the county decided to patch up the rough places and widen it at a
certain dangerous place. The gang is made up of twelve men, all
wearing black and white striped prison suits, and chained at the
ankles. There is a guard, with a gun, his eyes drawn to red slits by
the glare. The gang works all the day long, arriving huddled in the
prison cart soon after daybreak, and being driven off again in the
gray August twilight. All day there is the sound of the picks striking
into the clay earth, hard sunlight, the smell of sweat. And every day
there is music. One dark voice will start a phrase, half-sung, and like
a question. And after a moment another voice will join in, soon the
whole gang will be singing. The voices are dark in the golden glare,
the music intricately blended, both somber and joyful. The music
will swell until at last it seems that the sound does not come from

the twelve men on the gang, but from the earth itself, or the wide sky. It is music that causes the heart to broaden and the listener to grow cold with ecstasy and fright. Then slowly the music will sink down until at last there remains one lonely voice, then a great hoarse breath, the sun, the sound of the picks in the silence.

And what kind of gang is this that can make such music? Just twelve mortal men, seven of them black and five of them white boys from this county. Just twelve mortal men who are together.

The rhetorical stance or tone of this is wholly McCullers's, and is rather difficult to characterize. In context, its reverberation is extraordinary, working as it does against our incapacity to judge or even comprehend the grotesque tragedy of the doomed love between Miss Amelia Evans and Cousin Lymon, with its consequence in the curious flowering and subsequent demise of the sad café. We, as readers, also would rather love than be loved, a preference that, in the aesthetic register, becomes the defense of reading more intensely lest we ourselves be read, whether by ourselves or by others. The emotion released by the juxtaposition between the music and its origin in the chain gang is precisely akin to the affect arising from McCullers's vision of the tragic dignity of the death of love arising so incongruously from the story of Miss Amelia, Cousin Lymon, and the hideous Marvin Macy.

III

Rendering a canonical judgment upon the fiction of Carson McCullers is a problematical procedure for even the most generous of critics, could she or he be uncovered among the best informed students of American and of modern literature. The common reader has accepted McCullers rather more exuberantly than the recent critical tradition tends to do, and for the right reasons, so far as I can surmise. Few writers have expressed so vibrantly, and economically, a universal yearning for love, and simultaneously acknowledged the reality that such yearning almost inevitably wanes into the morasses of what Freud called the "erotic illusion." McCullers, by a discipline both subtle and open, confers an absolute aesthetic dignity upon even the most grotesque of our own desires and our ongoing illusions. That aesthetic dignity, sometimes precarious but always sustained, perhaps justifies her own yearning to claim Flaubert as one of her literary ancestors.

MARGUERITE YOUNG

Metaphysical Fiction

Carson McCullers's *The Member of the Wedding*, astutely and frugally designed, is a deceptive piece of writing, and its candor may betray the unwary
reader into accepting it as what it first seems, a study of turbulent adolescence.
Indeed, as such a study it has been most often reviewed, often by worldly reviewers who confess their weariness with the problems of a growing childhood,
even though such a childhood may be, as in this case, a complexus of unreal,
real, and surreal events, in a pattern which is itself as delusive as the dream of a
total happiness. Merely by thinking in terms of the individual childhood here
presented rather than in terms of the many and carefully erected symbols employed by the author in an argument concerned with man in his relation to
various kinds of reality, the reader may miss the importance of this curiously
spiritual book. Or he may wonder, especially if he is a parent, why Mrs. McCullers chose as her heroine a child who was more an individual than a type, a child
who was herself split into two warring beings though she sought for an eternal
harmony. Mrs. McCullers, sometimes depicted as a sensationalist revelling in the
grotesque, is more than that because she is first of all the poetic symbolist, a
seeker after those luminous meanings which always do transcend the boundaries
of the stereotyped, the conventional, and the so-called normal. Here, then, is a
fairly clear, explicit writing—explicit even in its use of the anomalous, the paradoxical, the amorphous—the confusions of life. Though its themes are romantic,
their working out is classically controlled. There is no wilderness for the reader
to get lost in, and if he is lost, it is perhaps because this writing does not weep,
gnash, wail, shout, wear its heart on its sleeve. It is rather like a chess game,

From *The Kenyon Review* 9, no. 1 (Winter 1947). © 1947 by Kenyon College.

where every move is a symbol and requires the reader's countermove. Many modern poems are of this order.

At first level, it is the story of a boy girl Frankie who, during a torrid summer, plans to join her brother's wedding, to get married to the two who are getting married, to belong, to be a member of something, to break down all barriers of atomic individualism, to be somehow intimately involved with all the intimate concerns of the happy human race. If Frankie can only crash in on this wedding of two other people to each other, being the third member, loving both, loved by both, even though she is excessive, why, then, there will be the kind of perfect happiness which man has always dreamed of, like a union of all the nations. Good-natured, proverb-haunted Berenice, the Negro cook who has brought up this semiorphaned child, assures her that her expectations can never be realized in actuality, that if they were realized, they would not be right, for her or the human race. What Frankie is dreaming of is possible only inside her own creative head, is nowhere else, is very far from possible. The purely imaginary goal is still a goal for Frankie, who cannot easily give up. She and Berenice sit discussing these crucial matters in endless, capacious luxury, capacious for them and for the reader, who can ponder as they ponder, think backward and forward. Then there is an audience, John Henry, aged six, who chimes in every once in a while and provides, in the drama, his own special, peculiar insights. He is beautifully described, once as a little blackbird running against the light. In fact, all three characters, all major, are treated with dignity and revealing tenderness, especially Berenice, whose blue glass eye is like Frankie's dream of the impossible wedding, a dream of almost heavenly harmony on earth. Berenice does not precisely dream of turning white, but her blue glass eye is a terrible commentary on the color line and the arbitrary divisions which shut off people from each other. All this book is a discussion of happiness, done as quietly as *Rasselas* by Dr. Johnson, and the conclusion is faintly similar to his. There are minor characters moving back and forth like the minor figures on a chessboard, in this case both cosmic and human. Nobody is ever disparaged. The Negro people are always people, thoughtful, mature, at home with Frankie who wants to belong to the human race, at home with John Henry, who is very soon to leave it and won't have much use for his little walking cane, a gift given to him most ironically on his death bed, given to him by optimistic Frankie, in fact.

By the above paragraph, I see the impossibility of describing the book without describing it in terms of its intricate symbols. Indeed, narrative and allegory are the two-headed flower growing from one stem, and if this is a "Pilgrim's Progress" backward to the cold and unintelligent and unintelligible universe suggested in Matthew Arnold's popular poem, it is still a pilgrim's progress, modernistic, aware of no simple definition of good and evil. One thing is always described in terms of another. The argument, though veiled by diverse imagery, is never lost. The imagery is functional. In fact, if there is any one statement to define Mrs. McCullers's position as a writer, it is not that she is merely the sensationalist but that she is also, like Sterne, the preacher, concerned with theories of knowledge—though the byplay of wit does not entice her away from the main themes. There is no lush undergrowth. Control is never absent. The framework is always visible.

People want to be told what they already believe, and Mrs. McCullers, in this case, is not telling most people what they already believe. Rather, she is continually questioning a great many complacent assumptions as to what is what, for she is too closely skeptical and analytical a writer to suppose that in the accepted platitudes lies truth. She weighs, she measures. Wild idealism does not carry her beyond the boundaries of a rigorous common sense world, partly for the reason that she finds the given world itself a sufficient phantasmagoria of lost events. Her attitude toward human nature is patient, behaviorist, clinical. Her writing, brooding and exploratory though it is, remains for these reasons as formal as a problem in geometry, though the perspectives bewilderingly and constantly shift. She sees life as impressionistic, but she herself is not the impressionist. She is a logician in an illogical realm.

Is there a given pattern in the nature of things, a music of the spheres, or was it all, as Mrs. McCullers implies, accident and chaos and fragment to begin with? Mrs. McCullers, speculative like her characters, dreams of an omniscient pattern but finds that such a pattern is rather more man's project than God's and that its realization may comprise another chaos. Then, too, there is the problem of how to make the inner world and the outer world conjoin, the problem immediately faced by Frankie, an anarchist in an old baseball cap. These three people, Frankie, John Henry, and Berenice sit around the kitchen table talking most musically while the green summer heat grows more and more oppressive around them. The focal subject is the impossible wedding, the illusory goal, out of which grow other illusory subjects, all related. John Henry draws crazy pictures on the wall. The piano tuner comes to tune the piano (perhaps next door), and the notes become a visible music climbing to the ceiling. And this is almost all that ever happens in the book but enough to keep the sensitive reader appalled to hear meaning after meaning dissolve, while the old problems continue. Is even green a color that can be said to be green to everybody? The metaphysical grows out of the immediate and returns to it, made no less rich because its origin is known. One of the most compelling passages is that in which Berenice tells of her search for happiness, which is exemplified to her in the person of her dead first husband. Berenice has been married three times, looking for him, three times unsatisfactorily. She married a man because he had a thumb like that of her dead first husband, another because he wore the coat which her dead first husband had worn and which she had pawned after his death and failed to claim, another because of a physical reason, her loneliness. Berenice says that her ideal world will be a world in which the blacks associate equally and freely with the whites and which will also include her dead first husband—though resurrection is not possible and might not even be feasible. Frankie's ideal world will be one where the wars are restricted to only an island for habitual warriors. It may even be a world made up of flickering cinematic figures. Berenice, Frankie, and John Henry, many-dimensioned, talking about what it means to be human, play in an alien system, all the while at a three-handed bridge game, emblematic of their plight. Some of the cards are, though they do not know it, missing from the beginning, maybe like those cards which God threw down at creation—and maybe that is why nothing ever turns out right, why there are expectation and disappointment. John Henry expresses his desire for an angular vision with which to read through and around the cards, a vision that can bend at will, for John Henry is of a philosophic turn of mind besides being a painter of crazy pictures.

At the end of the book, when the strange trilogy is broken up by death and moving away, it seems, in retrospect, a pattern as illusive and perfect as the wedding of three. It can never be recovered. The enchantment is implied in the writing but is not expressed by Frankie, who has come to the banal point of declaring that she just loves Michelangelo. Uncertainty seems to be her future. Either she will grow up, or she will not grow up.

TENNESSEE WILLIAMS

This Book: Reflections in a Golden Eye

This book, *Reflections in a Golden Eye*, is a second novel, and although its appreciation has steadily risen during the eight or nine years since its first appearance, it was then regarded as somewhat disappointing in the way that second novels usually are. When the book preceding a second novel has been very highly acclaimed, as was *The Heart Is a Lonely Hunter*, there is an inclination on the part of critics to retrench their favor, so nearly automatic and invariable a tendency that it can almost be set down as a physical law. But the reasons for failure to justly evaluate this second novel go beyond the common, temporal disadvantage that all second novels must suffer, and I feel that an examination of these reasons may be of considerably greater pertinence to our aim of suggesting a fresh evaluation.

To quote directly from book-notices that came out over a decade ago is virtually impossible, here in Rome where I am writing these comments, but I believe that I am safe in assuming that it was their identification of the author with a certain school of American writers, mostly of southern origin, that made her subject to a particular and powerful line of attack.

Even in the preceding book some readers must undoubtedly have detected a warning predisposition toward certain elements which are popularly known as "morbid." Doubtless there were some critics, as well as readers, who did not understand why Carson McCullers had elected to deal with a matter so unwholesome as the spiritual but passionate attachment that existed between a deaf-mute and a half-wit. But the tenderness of the book disarmed them. The depth and

From *Reflections in a Golden Eye*. © 1941 by Carson McCullers. New Directions, 1950. Originally entitled "This Book" (Introduction).

nobility of its compassion were so palpable that at least for the time being the charge of decadence had to be held in check. This forbearance was of short duration. In her second novel the veil of a subjective tenderness, which is the one quality of her talent which she has occasionally used to some excess, was drawn away. And the young writer suddenly flashed in their faces the cabalistic emblems of fellowship with a certain company of writers that the righteous "Humanists" in the world of letters regarded as most abhorrent and most necessary to expose and attack.

Not being a follower of literary journals, I am not at all sure what title has been conferred upon this group of writers by their disparaging critics, but for my own convenience I will refer to them as the Gothic school. It has a very ancient lineage, this school, but our local inheritance of its tradition was first brought into prominence by the early novels of William Faulkner, who still remains a most notorious and unregenerate member. There is something in the region, something in the blood and culture, of the southern state that has somehow made them the center of this Gothic school of writers. Certainly something more important than the influence of a single artist, Faulkner, is to be credited with its development, just as in France the Existentialist movement is surely attributable to forces more significant than the personal influence of Jean-Paul Sartre. There is actually a common link between the two schools, French and American, but characteristically the motor impulse of the French school is intellectual and philosophic while that of the American is more of an emotional and romantic nature. What is this common link? In my opinion it is most simply definable as a sense, an intuition, of an underlying dreadfulness in modern experience.

The question one hears most frequently about writers of the Gothic school is this little classic:

"Why do they write about such *dreadful* things?"

This is a question that escapes not only from the astonished lips of summer matrons who have stumbled into the odd world of William Faulkner, through some inadvertence or mischief at the lending-library, but almost as frequently and certainly more importantly, from the pens of some of the most eminent book-critics. If it were a solely and typically philistine manifestation, there would be no sense or hope in trying to answer it, but the fact that it is used as a major line of attack by elements that the artist has to deal with, critics, publishers, distributors, not to mention the reading public, makes it a question that we should try seriously to answer or at least understand.

The great difficulty of understanding, and communication, lies in the fact that we who are asked this question and those who ask it do not really inhabit the same universe.

You do not need to tell me that this remark smacks of artistic snobbism which is about as unattractive as any other form that snobbism can take. (If artists are snobs, it is much in the same humble way that lunatics are: not because they wish to be different, and hope and believe that they are, but because they are forever painfully struck in the face with the inescapable fact of their difference which makes them hurt and lonely enough to want to undertake the vocation of artists.)

It appears to me, sometimes, that there are only two kinds of people who live outside what E. E. Cummings has defined as "this socalled world of ours" — the artists and the insane. Of course there are those who are not practising artists and those who have not been committed to asylums, but who have enough of one or both magical elements, lunacy and vision, to permit them also to slip sufficiently apart from "this socalled world of ours" to undertake or accept an exterior view of it. But I feel that Mr. Cummings established a highly defensible point when he stated, at least by implication, that "the everyday humdrum world, which includes me and you and millions upon millions of men and women" is pretty largely something done with mirrors, and the mirrors are the millions of eyes that look at each other and things no more penetratingly than the physical senses allow. If they are conscious of there being anything to explore beyond this *soi-disant* universe, they comfortably suppose it to be represented by the mellow tones of the pipe-organ on Sundays.

In expositions of this sort it is sometimes very convenient to invent an opposite party to an argument, as Mr. Cummings did in making the remarks I have quoted. Such an invented adversary might say to me at this point:

"I have read some of these books, like this one here, and I think they're sickening and crazy. I don't know why anybody should want to write about such diseased and perverted and fantastic creatures and try to pass them off as representative members of the human race! That's how I feel about it. But I do have this sense you talk about, as much as you do or anybody else, this sense of fearfulness or dreadfulness or whatever you want to call it. I read the newspapers and I think it's all pretty awful. I think the atom bomb is awful and I think that the confusion of the world is awful. I think that cancer is fearful, and I certainly don't look forward to the idea of dying, which I think is dreadful. I could go on forever, or at least indefinitely, giving you a list of things that I think are dreadful. And isn't that having what you call the Sense of Dreadfulness or something?"

My hesitant answer would be—"Yes, and no. Mostly no."

And then I would explain a little further, with my usual awkwardness at exposition:

"All of these things that you list as dreadful are parts of the visible, sensible phenomena of every man's experience or knowledge, but the true sense of dread is not a reaction to anything sensible or visible or even, strictly, materially, *knowable*. But rather it's a kind of spiritual intuition of something almost too incredible and shocking to talk about, which underlies the whole so-called thing. It is the incommunicable something that we shall have to call *mystery* which is so inspiring of dread among these modern artists that we have been talking about. . . ."

Then I pause, looking into the eyes of my interlocutor which I hope are beginning to betray some desire to believe me, and I say to him, "Am I making any better sense?"

"Maybe. But I can see it's an effort!"

"My friend, you have me where the hair is short."

"But you know, you still haven't explained why these writers have to write about crazy people doing terrible things!"

"You mean the externals they use?"

" 'Externals?' "

"You are objecting to their choice of symbols."

"Symbols, are they?"

"Of course. Art is made out of symbols the way your body is made out of vital tissue."

"Then why have they got to use—?"

"Symbols of the grotesque and the violent? Because a book is short and a man's life is long."

"That I don't understand."

"Think it over."

"You mean it's got to be more concentrated?"

"Exactly. The awfulness has to be compressed."

"But can't a writer ever get the same effect without using such God damn awful subjects?"

"I believe one writer did. The greatest of modern times, James Joyce. He managed to get the whole sense of awfulness without resorting to externals that departed on the surface from the ordinary and the familiar. But he wrote very long books, when he accomplished this incredibly difficult thing, and also he used a device that is known as the interior monologue which only he and one other great modern writer could employ without being excessively tiresome."

"What other?"

"Marcel Proust. But Proust did not ever quite dare to deliver the message of Absolute Dread. He was too much of a physical coward. The atmosphere of his work is rather womb-like. The flight into protection is very apparent."

"I guess we've talked long enough. Don't you have to get back to your subject now?"

"I have just about finished with my subject, thanks to you."

"Aren't you going to make a sort of statement that adds it up?"

"Neatly? Yes. Maybe I'd better try: here it is: *Reflections in a Golden Eye* is one of the purest and most powerful of those works which are conceived in that Sense of The Awful which is the desperate black root of nearly all significant modern art, from the *Guernica* of Picasso to the cartoons of Charles Addams. Is that all right?"

"I have quit arguing with you. So long."

It is true that this book lacks somewhat the thematic magnitude of the *Chasseur Solitaire*, but there is an equally important respect in which it is superior.

The first novel had a tendency to overflow in places as if the virtuosity of the young writer had not yet fallen under her entire control. But in the second there is an absolute mastery of design. There is a lapidary precision about the structure of this second book. Furthermore I think it succeeds more perfectly in establishing its own reality, in creating a world of its own, and this is something that primarily distinguishes the work of a great artist from that of a professional writer. In this book there is perhaps no single passage that assaults the heart so mercilessly as that scene in the earlier novel where the deaf-mute Singer stands at night outside the squalid flat that he had formerly occupied with the crazed and now dying Antonapolous. The acute tragic sensibility of scenes like that occurred more frequently in *The Heart Is a Lonely Hunter*. Here the artistic climate is more austere. The tragedy is more distilled: a Grecian purity cools it, the eventually overwhelming impact is of a more reflective order. The key to this deliberate difference is implicit in the very title of the book. Discerning critics should have found it the opposite of a disappointment since it exhibited the one attribute which had yet to be shown in Carson McCullers's stunning array of gifts: the gift of mastery over a youthful lyricism.

I will add, however, that this second novel is still not her greatest; it is surpassed by *The Member of the Wedding*, her third novel, which combined the heart-breaking tenderness of the first with the sculptural quality of the second. But this book is in turn surpassed by a somewhat shorter work. I am speaking of *The Ballad of the Sad Café*, which is assuredly among the masterpieces of our language in the form of the novella. It has appeared, so far, only in the pages of a magazine of fashion and in an otherwise rather undistinguished anthology, which is now out of print. It is at present obtainable only after diligent search among the stalls of dealers in old magazines and remainders. But as I write these comments I am assured that it is soon to be re-issued in a volume of short stories.

During the two years that I have spent mostly abroad I have been impressed by the disparity that exists between Carson McCullers's reputation at home and in Europe. Translation serves as a winnowing process. The lesser and more derivative talents that have boisterously flooded our literary scene, with reputations inflated by professional politics and by shrewd commercial promotion, have somewhat obscured at home the position of more authentic talents. But in Europe the name of Carson McCullers is where it belongs, among the four or five pre-eminent figures in contemporary American writing.

Carson McCullers does not work rapidly. She is not coerced by the ridiculous popular idea that a good novelist turns out a book once a year. As long as five years elapsed between her second full-length novel and her third. I understand now that she has begun to work upon another. There could be no better literary news for any of us who have found, as I have found in her work, such intensity and nobility of spirit as we have not had in our prose-writing since Herman Melville. In the meantime she should be reassured by the constantly more abundant evidence that the work she has already accomplished, such as this work, is not eclipsed by time but further illumined.

GORE VIDAL

Carson McCullers's
Clock Without Hands

It is hard to believe that twenty-one years have passed since *The Heart Is a Lonely Hunter*, the first novel of Carson McCullers, was published. For those of us who arrived on the scene in the war years, McCullers was *the* young writer. She was an American legend from the beginning, which is to say that her fame was as much the creation of publicity as of talent. The publicity was the work of those fashion magazines where a dish of black-eyed peas can be made to seem the roe of some rare fish, photographed by Avedon; yet McCullers's dreaming, androgynous face in its ikon elegance subtly confounded the chic of the lingerie ads all about her. For unlike other "legends," her talent was as real as her face. Though she was progenitress to much "southern writing" (one can name a dozen writers who would not exist in the way they do if she had not written in the way she did), she had a manner all her own. Her prose was chaste and severe, and realistic in its working out of narrative. I suspect that of all the southern writers, she is the most apt to endure, though her vision is by no means as large or encompassing as that, say, of Faulkner, whom she has the grace to resemble not at all.

Southern writing—we have had such a lot of it in the last thirty years! Novelist after novelist has come to us out of the South, and there is no doubt that the southern gift for the novel is as real as the southern town, where family groups are more concentrated and less mobile than in the North. The Industrial Revolution was a long time coming South, and until recently the young southerner was not apt to be thrown into the commercial world quite so soon or so fiercely as his

From *Rocking the Boat.* © 1956–1962 by Gore Vidal. Little, Brown and Company, 1962.

northern counterpart. But above all, there are the stories. Southerners talk and talk, tell and tell. In the rural areas, spinning long intricate stories of character is still a social skill. Up North, everyday conversation is mostly the repeating of the generalized anecdote: "You know the one about this man who met this woman who. . . ." In the South, it is: "When your cousin Hattie, she was Eula's step-sister, which makes her second cousin to James Edward, had to quit her job at the Court House after the fire, she met the Tutwiler boy, the one who tried to kill his father Memorial Day. . . ." They talk in chronicles and annals. They talk in novels. It is not that life is more interesting in the South than elsewhere. Rather, it is the pleasure the people take in talking of neighbors and kin; the long memories and the delight in pondering that vast web of relationship which for three centuries has spun itself (white web!) over the red earth of what was wilderness.

From the beginning the South was provincial and middle-class. Its delusions of aristocracy began before the Civil War, when the novels of Sir Walter Scott took the plantation owners—and the not too many others who could read —by storm. Deliberately and disastrously, they modeled themselves on the folk of Scott's imagination. Faulkner's Sartoris is drawn not from fact but from Scott. Yet this lunatic dream of blue blood and inner grace is useful to an imaginative child. I doubt if there is a southerner alive who has not been told in youth by at least one female relative, "Never forget *who* you are!" And yet who is this *who*? Just a plain middle-class child, usually of a lower-income group, with nothing grander in his family tree than a doctor or a lawyer or maybe an itinerant preacher. Yet to be told that you are, through blood, a Somebody starts a magic in the veins, starts dreams of empire and dominion, dreams of making, and, if the balance is right, in time the dream becomes reality and art *is* made.

The first thing to remark in McCullers is her style. From Wolfe to Faulkner, most southern writing has tended to windy rhetoric of the "lost, lost and by the wind grieved" sort which I find entirely detestable. I can read very little of Wolfe, and much of the admirable Faulkner is ruined for me by that terrible gaseous prose (he went the length of *Requiem for a Nun* obsessively using "euphemistic" for "euphonious"). McCullers writes an exact prose closer to the Flaubert of *Un Cœur Simple* than to *Absalom, Absalom!* But her material is intensely southern. Although she has had at times a passion for the extreme situation and the gratuitous act (*The Ballad of the Sad Café, Reflections in a Golden Eye*), whose intent I sometimes question, her means have always saved her. She gets entirely within the event told. There is never a false note. Technically, it is breathtaking to watch her set a scene and then dart from character to character, opening up in a line, a phrase, a life. It is marvelous, but . . .

But. Twenty-one years is a long time. *The Member of the Wedding*, her latest novel until now, was published in 1946. During those fifteen years other writers have come and gone. New attitudes, new follies, new perceptions have occurred to us. But most important, the world of the private vision which was her domain has been more and more intruded upon by the public world which threatens to destroy, literally, the actual world. Worse, though it may not do this final thing, the threat of extinction has made many doubt the worth of art. If the planet becomes an empty desert, why make anything, knowing it will soon be no more than a grain or two in the never-to-be-noticed dust? Not every writer of course has this apocalyptic vision, nor does a writer necessarily find the thought of the world's end any reason for not making what he wants to make in the present, which is all. But that ugly final thing *is* there, public and menacing and chilling the day. It is hard not to take it into account.

In her new novel, *Clock Without Hands*, Carson McCullers acknowledges the public world for the first time in her work. Though her response is uneasy and uncertain, it is good to note that she writes as well as ever, with all the old clarity and fine tension. But the book is odd, and it is so because what has always been the most private of responses has been rudely startled and bemused by the world outside. The changing South. The Supreme Court Decision. Integration. The aviator as new man. All these things crop up unexpectedly in her narrative. One cannot say she handles these things badly; it is just that they do not quite fit her story of a gross old man (judge and white supremacist), his grandson (adolescent air voyager, perceptive), a dying druggist named Malone (who unexpectedly tries to stop a lynching), a colored youth (mad with hurt and self-delusion: is he really Marion Anderson's son left by her in a pew of a church in this Georgia town?). The four characters interact. They are explored. They come alive. Yet one is not convinced by the story told. Symbolically, is it true or merely pat?

At the book's end, the old judge, enraged by the Supreme Court's decision, goes on radio to denounce the Court, but in his dottiness and great age he cannot recall anything to say except, word for word, the Gettysburg Address. Are we to take that as the South's last gasp as a new order begins? If so, I don't believe it. McCullers of course is free to make whatever she wants of a public situation. One quarrels not with her view of things, which is after all intuitive not liberal, but with the effect publicness has had on her art. Everything is thrown slightly out of kilter. She is not the only writer to suffer in this way. More and more of our private artists have fallen silent in the last twenty years, unable to cope with a world which has thrust itself upon the imagination like some clumsy-hooved animal loose in a garden. But even this near failure of McCullers is marvelous to read, and her genius for prose remains one of the few satisfying achievements of our second-rate culture.

OLIVER EVANS

The Achievement
of Carson McCullers

Carson McCullers is quite possibly the most controversial living American writer. The controversy began in 1940, with the publication of *The Heart Is a Lonely Hunter*, and has continued ever since: it has recently received fresh stimulus from the publication, last September, of her fifth novel, *Clock Without Hands*.

Reviewing this controversy, one notices that, with one or two exceptions, the censure has come from professional book reviewers while the praise has come either from other novelists (and a few poets and playwrights) or from a group of critics whom, for want of a better label, I shall call academic—that is, men whose profession is teaching and whose avocation is scholarly criticism. There is therefore some evidence for believing that Mrs. McCullers is both a "writer's writer" and one whose work requires, or at least lends itself to, a considerable amount of explication—more, at any rate, than the popular reviewer, either for reasons of space or because he lacks the proper literary background, is prepared to supply. I think this is emphatically the case, though I am by no means certain that it explains the controversy. The truth, I suspect, is that Mrs. McCullers's is a very special sensibility with which many readers, even highly cultivated readers, are, for some reason, simply unable to establish a rapport. Mrs. McCullers is not unique among authors in this respect (the case of Ford Madox Ford, a very different kind of writer, is somewhat similar), and in a sense the phenomenon is proof of her individuality and originality as an artist.

From *The English Journal* 51, no. 5 (May 1962). © 1962 by the National Council of Teachers of English.

THE METHOD OF ALLEGORY

It is impossible to understand Mrs. McCullers's work unless one realizes that she conceives of fiction chiefly as parable. The reader who concerns himself exclusively with the realistic level of her stories will never fully appreciate them, though he may be momentarily diverted. The narrative burden of her work is always secondary to the allegorical: she is in this sense a didactic writer, for she does not write to entertain but to teach, and what she has to teach are those truths about human nature that she has learned from her experience, which is profound, and from her observation, which, at the same time that it is compassionate, is penetrating to the point of clairvoyance. It is in no narrower sense than this that she may be thought of as being didactic, for she has no particular ax to grind, no program to push, no *specific* reforms to recommend: her concern is with nothing less than the soul of man.

These truths with which Mrs. McCullers has been concerned in her writing do not always flatter the reader; on the contrary, they are—as we shall see—of a generally melancholy nature, and here is perhaps another reason why many readers have been unwilling to acknowledge them. (The reluctance with which they have viewed them, however, may well be the measure of their suspicion that they are sound.) Be that as it may, the point I should like to make here is that though Mrs. McCullers's truths may not be comfortable to live with, and though they may not even be truths, they are nevertheless the convictions at which she has arrived out of her experience, and it is with them that she is primarily concerned in her narratives, which are to that extent allegories and parables.

Now the method of allegory involves a certain sacrifice: in proportion as the characters are abstracted, they tend to lose their humanity, becoming symbols rather than people, so that perhaps the commonest complaint against allegory is that the characters do not seem like "real people." Readers should bear in mind, however, that this is a criticism of the method rather than of the particular work which employs it: one either approves of abstraction or disapproves of it, likes allegory or dislikes it. The mutilations and aberrations of Mrs. McCullers's characters are not gratuitous but are essential to the dramatization of her thesis, and she is not attempting to create a "true picture" of life in the realistic sense at all, but in another, more indirect and possibly more artistic (to the extent that calculation is involved in a work of art) sense: that is, the symbolic.

I would be embarrassed to stress so obvious a point if it did not seem to me the best way both of accounting for the peculiar difficulty of Mrs. McCullers's work and of assessing her achievement as an artist. The fact is that this writer is so gifted technically, so thoroughly in command of the devices of realism (her dialogue is a good example), that it is a constant temptation to read her largely on that level, overlooking the allegorical scheme of which one must be everywhere conscious in her work. It is Mrs. McCullers's ambiguous achievement that no other living American writer of allegorical fiction has mastered the techniques of realism quite so well: I say ambiguous because I am not at all certain that it has worked to her aesthetic advantage, since even the most discriminating reader can be distracted from the proper subject of a book by a display of surface brilliance—especially if it occurs in flashes, some brighter than others.

The relationship, in allegory, between the literal and symbolic levels constitutes one of the most delicate problems in literary art, as there are innumerable failures—some of them magnificent failures—to testify, and it is the only problem that, for all her astonishing virtuosity, Mrs. McCullers has not yet finally solved. Granted the difficulties that inhere in the abstraction process, the most successful allegories are those in which the literal level, however simple, is coherent but is never permitted to triumph at the expense of the allegorical. In Kafka, for example—a pure allegorist—the realistic level is negligible; it is there, but the reader understands from the first that it is not to be taken as seriously as the symbolic, and though Kafka's characters do not have the human interest that Mrs. McCullers's often do, they are nevertheless more effective, for that reason, as symbols. The same is true, to a somewhat less extent, of Camus. Only the very greatest artists can succeed, at the same time they are concerned primarily with allegorical meanings, in creating characters who are interesting in their own right. Hawthorne did it in *The Scarlet Letter*, in the character of Hester Prynne, but in his other work even Hawthorne was by no means invariably successful. Melville did it in *Billy Budd*, an otherwise badly written book, the product of his senescence, and failed to do it in *Moby Dick*, the product of his prime. Mrs. McCullers herself has done it—once, in *The Member of the Wedding*, which I do not think is on that account her best novel—and I can think of no other living American author who has, unless it be Paul Bowles in that remarkable little story that almost no one seems to have read more than once, "The Fourth Day Out from Santa Cruz."

But in some of Mrs. McCullers's work—I will not say all—one is uneasily aware of a struggle between the two levels, and I think this explains the unevenness that many readers have found in it. I am particularly conscious of this struggle in her first novel, *The Heart Is a Lonely Hunter*, and her latest, *Clock Without Hands*. It is as though Camus were attempting to write, here and there, in the style of Flaubert—and succeeding. (Flaubert, by the way, is one of Mrs. McCullers's favorite authors.) The novels of what we may term her "middle period" do not suffer from this defect, or suffer from it so slightly that we are scarcely conscious of it: the literal levels in *Reflections in a Golden Eye* and *The Ballad of the Sad Café*, while coherent, are so improbable that few readers have any difficulty separating them from the allegorical. I should say that, as pure allegory, *The Ballad of the Sad Café* is Mrs. McCullers's most successful book, and I quite agree with Mr. Irving Howe when he calls it "one of the finest novels ever written by an American" (*New York Times Book Review*, September 17, 1961). If I admire it more than *The Member of the Wedding*, and I believe I do, it is in spite of the fact that in the latter work Mrs. McCullers has wrought the miracle of creating a character that is as effective humanly as she is symbolically —Frankie Addams.

HUMAN LOVE AND LONELINESS

The themes with which Mrs. McCullers was mainly concerned in the first decade of her career are the spiritual isolation of the individual and the power of love to free him from this condition. Ordinary verbal communication results in failure; it is only through ideal communication, or love, that men can hope to escape from their cells. In *The Heart Is a Lonely Hunter*, she dramatizes this idea by causing her protagonist, Singer, to be a deaf mute, and it is not in spite of this limitation but because of it that his experience in love is the only one, of the several which are depicted in the novel, that is satisfactory—and it is only relatively so, since the object of his love, the half-witted Antonapoulos, does not reciprocate it and soon dies. The melancholy message here is that, while love is the only force that can unite men, love is never completely mutual and is subject to time, diminishing with the death of the love object. The single consolation is that love, while it lasts, is beneficial to the lover, affording him temporary relief from his solitude.

This same idea was presented, somewhat more obliquely, in the second novel, *Reflections in a Golden Eye*, where spiritual isolation is symbolized in the character of Captain Penderton, who is a homosexual, a sadist, a kleptomaniac, and a drug addict; and in *The Member of the Wedding*, whose protagonist is an adolescent girl, Frankie Addams, who feels herself too old to associate with children and too young to mingle confidently with adults: she is "an unjoined person who hangs around in doorways" —that is, on the threshold of things, never really inside nor out. But it was in *The Ballad of the Sad Café* that the related themes of spiritual isolation and the nature and function of love received their fullest and most mature treatment. It is the saddest of Mrs. McCullers's novels at the same time that it is the most nearly perfect, with something of the formal beauty of a Bach fugue, for in it she reaches the profoundly pessimistic conclusion that "The state of being beloved is intolerable to many. . . . The beloved fears and hates the lover." Her protagonist here is a lonely manlike giantess, Amelia Evans, who falls in love with a dwarf who is also homosexual, hunchbacked, and tubercular, thus illustrating yet another thesis of the author, that "The most outlandish people can be the stimulus for love. . . . The value and quality of any love is determined solely by the lover. Instead of returning her love, however, the dwarf maliciously solicits the attentions of Amelia's former husband, an ex-convict, and the two revenge themselves upon her by running off together—but not before they have wrecked her place of business, stolen her belongings, and attempted to poison her.

There is a terrible finality about the vision of life set forth in *The Ballad of the Sad Café*, and one wondered if the author had not said all she had to say on the theme of human love and loneliness. Seven years of silence seemed to confirm this suspicion, and when the play, *The Square Root of Wonderful*, finally appeared, her admirers read it eagerly to see if she had chosen another theme— or rather to see if (Mrs. McCullers being the kind of writer she is) another theme had chosen her. They were encouraged in this expectation by a statement in the preface:

> In *The Square Root of Wonderful* I recognize many of the compulsions that made me write this play. My husband wanted to be a writer and his failure in that was one of the disappointments that led to his death. When I started *The Square Root of Wonderful* my mother was very ill and after a few months she died. I wanted to recreate my mother—to remember her tranquil beauty and sense of joy in life. So, unconsciously, the life-death theme of *The Square Root of Wonderful* emerged.

The play's protagonist is a young woman, Mollie Lovejoy, who has been twice married to and divorced from the same man, a once-famous writer who, after the failure of his latest play, has attempted suicide and is convalescing in a rest home. Mollie has meanwhile fallen in love with an architect, John, and is on the point of marrying him when Philip, her ex-husband, returns. The two men are opposites: John is dull but strong, and he worships Mollie; Philip is weak and has learned to use his weakness to advantage with women, but he is charming and perceptive. He does not love Mollie—it is made clear that he is incapable of loving anyone—but he needs her desperately and insists that she love *him*. In a moment of weakness she yields to him once more, but repents almost immediately, and when Philip realizes he has lost her for good he drowns himself; Mollie is then free to marry John. Other characters are Mollie's thirteen-year-old son, Paris; Mother Lovejoy, a fatuous but domineering woman whose mismanagement of Philip's childhood is responsible for many of his problems (he loathes her, calling her to her face a "babbling old horror"); and Sister, her daughter, a homely spinster who compensates for the drabness of her situation by inventing fantasies involving Latin lovers.

The play, it will be seen, ends on a "positive" note, even if it does not have the conventional happy ending (Mrs. McCullers in her preface calls it a tragi-comedy), and is generally different from her earlier work. There are, to be sure, certain correspondences: the irrationality of love is again insisted upon ("Love is very much like witches and ghosts, and childhood," Mollie says. "When it speaks to you you have to answer, and you have to go wherever it tells you."); so also is the loneliness that springs from an incapacity for love ("I feel surrounded by a zone of loneliness," Philip complains); and Sister's fantasies remind us of Mick's, in *The Heart Is a Lonely Hunter*, and of Frankie's in *The Member of the Wedding*. But the life–death theme, obviously related to that of loneliness and love, is here the important thing. Philip, in his inability to love, personifies the death principle, or, in Freudian terms, the death wish (it is significant that he takes his own life), and Mollie, who is capable of loving more than one man simulta-neously, personifies the vital principle. Life triumphs over death in the play, and in a sense it is the triumph of the mediocre over the exceptional, for Philip is cer-tainly the most interesting character in the play: the healthy vulgarity of Mollie reminds one of Stella, in *A Streetcar Named Desire*, and indeed the two plays have very similar conclusions.

A preoccupation with the meaning of time is also evident in *The Square Root of Wonderful*. The relation of time to love is obvious: it is the Great Enemy of love as it is of life, of which love is the surest sign and the happiest manifesta-tion. In as early a story as "The Sojourner" (1950), Ferris presses his little boy close to him "as though an emotion as protean as his love could dominate the pulse of time," and it is time, and time alone, that enables Singer to forget his powerful love for Antonapoulos in *The Heart Is a Lonely Hunter*. But in relation to loneliness, time takes on another significance. Thus, in *The Square Root of Wonderful*, Mollie remarks, apropos of the grandfather clock, "It reminds me of peace and family," and Philip replies: "It puts me in mind of time. You were winding it when I came back. Busily, busily winding time. I hate clocks." Mollie merely says, "It has a lovely chime." Philip does not dislike clocks because they remind him that time is running out; he dislikes them for the opposite reason, because they remind him of how much time he will have to kill before he finds release from his loneliness: for him, as for all unhappy people, clocks do not run too fast but too slow. Time passes quickly for the lover, and in that sense may be thought of as a traitor and an enemy, but it is an even greater enemy to the loveless.

As a play, *The Square Root of Wonderful* has a good many faults: there are too many "gag lines" on a rather low level of humor; the characterization of John is thin, and that of Paris inconsistent (imagine a twelve-year-old, normal in other respects, saying: "Mother, you eavesdrop and read diaries. I don't respect anybody who reads diaries. Sly people."); and Mother Lovejoy bears too obvious a resemblance to Amanda Wingfield in *The Glass Menagerie*—she boasts of the many gentlemen callers she received before marrying her husband, who (like Amanda's) later walked out on her, and her relationship to Sister is identical with Amanda's to Laura, just as her relationship to Philip is identical with Amanda's to Tom. (Mrs. McCullers's friendship with Tennessee Williams, as she observes in the preface, has profoundly affected both her life and her work.) But it is a better play than the reviewers, by and large, gave her credit for—they were merely courteous, and very few of them bothered to look beneath its surface. And it is important in that it represents a widening of the author's perspective to include other metaphysical problems than those with which she had previously been occupied.

CLOCK WITHOUT HANDS

Clock Without Hands has four main characters: J. T. Malone, a forty-year-old pharmacist; his friend, Judge Clane, a militant white supremacist, age eighty-five; the Judge's grandson, Jester, who is nineteen; and a blue-eyed Negro youth named Sherman Pew. When the novel opens, Malone has been told by his physician that he has leukemia; though he knows he must die he does not know when, and is thus like a man watching a clock without hands. Malone is a sheeplike man who has allowed his life to be managed for him by other people, and, in a flash of self-knowledge born of the realization of his approaching death, he realizes that he has never really lived: how then, he wonders, can he die? He is determined to acquire an identity in the few months remaining to him so that his life, before it ends, will have some meaning. Jester, likewise, is in search of an identity: he has not yet decided what he wants to be in life; though he has many passing interests he feels no "call" for any particular vocation, and the anonymity of his situation is symbolized in the fact that he has never known either of his parents, his father having committed suicide shortly before his mother died in giving him birth. Still a third character, Sherman, is seeking to know himself, and in his case the fact coincides directly with the symbol, as he was a foundling who received his surname from the circumstance of his having been abandoned in a church.

The mystery surrounding Sherman's parentage adds much to the interest of the plot on a realistic level, and it is connected with the mystery surrounding the suicide of Jester's father. Jester finally learns from the Judge that he and his son had not seen eye-to-eye on the race problem (neither do Jester and the Judge, incidentally), and that his father, a lawyer, had fallen in love with one of his clients, a white woman whose Negro lover was on trial for murdering her husband. Jester's father tried to convince the jury that the killing was in self defense (which it was), but the trial, at which the Judge presided, proved a mockery of justice: the Negro was hanged, and the woman, who had refused to testify against him, cursed Jester's father on her deathbed—she died in childbirth shortly after the trial—for losing the case. Maddened by his failure, by the injustice of the incident, by the frustration of his love, and by the death of his client, who never guessed that he took more than a professional interest in the case, Jester's father shot himself. Sherman Pew was this woman's son by her Negro lover.

Jester's inherent liberalism is strengthened by the knowledge that social injustice has been partly to blame for the tragedy of his father's life, and he resolves to become a lawyer himself and take up the battle where his father left off: his life thus achieves moral direction. Sherman is not so fortunate; he is to find his identity in martyrdom, for when he moves into a white neighborhood his house is bombed, and, though he has been warned by Jester, he refuses to flee and loses his life. As for Malone, who has taken orders all his life, his opportunity comes when, at a drawing of lots to determine who shall bomb Sherman's house, the job falls to him and he refuses it. Shortly after this he dies with the consolation of having made a moral choice for himself and thus of having lived at last, however briefly.

THE SEARCH FOR THE SELF

In all of Mrs. McCullers's earlier work—even in *The Square Root of Wonderful*—she was concerned with the loneliness that results from a lack of rapport with other individuals; in *Clock Without Hands* she is concerned with the loneliness that results from a lack of rapport with the self. The search for self is the theme of her latest novel, and in its insistence upon the necessity for moral engagement and upon the importance of choice one recognizes the impact of existential doctrine: the "existential crisis," indeed, is at the very center of the book. (The book that Malone chooses to read in the hospital is Kierkegaard's *Sickness Unto Death*, and the sentence in it that most impresses him is: "The greatest danger, that of losing one's own self, may pass off quietly as if it were nothing; every other loss, that of an arm, a leg, five dollars, a wife, etc., is sure to be noticed.")

I have shown how the theme of identity is related to that of loneliness, and they are both related to the time phenomenon: loss of identity results in loneliness, and when one is lonely time, as we have noted, passes with maddening slowness. It is for this reason that Malone, while he is waiting for his death—or rather for the moment of free engagement which will give meaning to his life— complains of a "zone of loneliness" (the same phrase that Philip uses in *The Square Root of Wonderful*) that the summer seems interminable to Jester, lounging in his grandfather's big house; and that Sherman, in spite of the job the Judge gives him as his "private amanuensis," is horribly bored and haunted toward the end by a feeling that he must "do something." The old Judge is lonely also, not because he lacks identity but because when his wife, whom he loved sincerely, died, his capacity for love died with her. He does not love his grandson so much as he is hurt by the knowledge (which he tries to conceal from himself) that Jester can no longer love *him*.

The theme of identity is also related to that of ideal love. Like Frankie in *The Member of the Wedding*, both Jester and Sherman yearn to identify themselves with something bigger than themselves and outside themselves, which is merely another way of saying that they are unconsciously seeking a love object. This is symbolized on the literal level by the fact that Jester cannot love his grandfather and that Sherman, longing for a mother, invents a fantasy that she is Marian Anderson. The same is true of Malone, of whom it is significant that he cannot love his wife: he is seeking an ideal love, not a physical one (like Frankie, he does not wish to be joined to any particular person but to *that which joins all people*—as Frankie puts it, "the 'we' of me.") It is by thus identifying themselves with something larger than themselves—in this case the ideal of social justice— that all of them become conscious of their individual identities.

The search for identity parallels the search for ideal love, but in *Clock Without Hands*, as elsewhere in Mrs. McCullers's work, love on the physical level is doomed to disappointment: Malone's daughter, Ellen, loves Jester, who is scarcely aware of her existence; Jester is secretly in love with Sherman, who constantly mistreats him; and Sherman worships another Negro, Zippo, whose "house guest" he is and who mistreats *him*. The pattern is even carried back to an earlier generation, for it will be remembered that Jester's father was in love with his client, who cursed him with her dying breath. Here, as in *The Ballad of the Sad Café*, the beloved "fears and hates" the lover: when Jester attempts to kiss Sherman, the caress is returned with a blow, and when Malone's wife makes advances to him he is repelled and rushes from the house. And just as Mrs. McCullers in her other novels was careful to select characters between whom any physical union was out of the question (like the manlike Amelia and the homosexual dwarf), she has here been at pains to depict another impossible situation, since Sherman is not only of the same sex as Jester but is also a Negro. There is also in this novel the same peculiar mixture of love and pity that characterized the relationship of Singer and Antonapoulos in *The Heart Is a Lonely*

Hunter; of Mrs. Langdon and Anacleto in *Reflections in a Golden Eye*; of Martin Meadows and Emily in the short story "A Domestic Dilemma"; and of Amelia and the dwarf in *The Ballad of the Sad Café*. For Mrs. Malone's ill-timed advances are made in the knowledge that her husband has not long to live, and Jester feels sorry for Sherman because of his race.

Yet another familiar idea in *Clock Without Hands* is that illusions are necessary to enable men to endure their existence. Just as Mick dreams of becoming a concert pianist in *The Heart Is a Lonely Hunter* and Frankie dreams of traveling around the world in *The Member of the Wedding*, and just as Sister in *The Square Root of Wonderful* chooses her lovers from the Mediterranean area, so here Jester dreams of saving Marilyn Monroe from an avalanche in Switzerland and riding down Broadway in a blizzard of ticker tape, while Sherman convinces himself that his real mother is Marian Anderson and writes her letters that are never answered. Even the old Judge has his dreams, which center about the restoration of Confederate currency by the federal government. As for Malone, bored with his wife and work, he daydreams constantly, and his situation reminds us of Frankie Addams's: it is, in fact, the situation of most men, forced into an unhappy compromise between the ideal romantic relationships for which they long and those humdrum and unsatisfactory substitutes which are available to them. Malone, indeed, is Everyman, with Everyman's share of faults but also with his dignity and capacity for the moral life. And of course the shadow of his impending death is the same shadow under which all men labor: to this extent we are all watching a "clock without hands."

I have only hinted at the extraordinary richness of this novel, which is full of incidental meanings and of the wonderful insights and observations that we have come to expect of its author ("The laughter of disaster does not stop easily, and so they laughed for a long time, each for his own disaster"). It is full, too, of her powerful compassion, a compassion that embraces even the dishonest old Judge, who reads the Kinsey Report behind the covers of Gibbon's *Decline and Fall of the Roman Empire* but sees that it is banned from the public library. The Judge is marvelously real; he is Mrs. McCullers's best character to date, and I almost wish that this were not the case, for in no sense is he the protagonist of the book. The author has allowed herself to be carried away in the process of creating a character who, for all his lifelikeness, is minor to her essential purpose. The realistic level of the novel is concerned with his activities, and they are so engrossing in themselves that they detract from the primary themes, which are expressed in terms of allegory. The chief defects of *Clock Without Hands* are thus defects of emphasis and proportion.

I do not think I overstate the case when I say that Carson McCullers is probably the best allegorical writer on this side of the Atlantic since Hawthorne and Melville. Her writing is almost never peripheral, as Faulkner's often is; it goes straight to the heart of its subject, and it rarely fumbles. It is ironical that her gift for realism, especially in dialogue and characterization, has operated in her case less as a blessing than as a curse. As I see it, Mrs. McCullers is now faced with the choice of returning to pure allegory like *The Ballad of the Sad Café* or of writing a straight realistic novel. There is still a third alternative—of creating a main character who, like Frankie Addams, will be as convincing as a human being as she is effective allegorically.

KLAUS LUBBERS

The Necessary Order

For the general reading public, the name of Carson McCullers has come to be associated with Frankie Addams, the heroine of her most popular book *The Member of the Wedding* (1946) which was later made into a favorably received play and a successful motion picture. But it is rather on her other fiction—*The Heart Is a Lonely Hunter* (1940), *Reflections in a Golden Eye* (1941) and *The Ballad of the Sad Café* (1951)—that her slowly but steadily increasing critical reputation rests. After the lapse of more than a decade between the appearance of her latest novella and the publication of a new novel, *Clock Without Hands*, in September 1961, it is time to revaluate her achievement.

Together with such other writers as Katherine Anne Porter and Eudora Welty, Mrs. McCullers forms a southern triad that has carried on and modified the basic Faulknerian themes of lust, disease, mutilation, defeat, idiocy and death. All of these notes, with a shift in emphasis, are played in her fiction over and again: disease crops up in the form of permanent distortion in the figures of the cretin, the crippled and the incurable; the theme of death is effectively pitted against that of adolescence; the idea of defeat is narrowed down to personal disillusion resulting from tragic initiation into life or from the failure of a mis-directed lifework—it does not carry the historical implications as in Faulkner's concept of the past bearing down heavily upon the present; mutilation is the fate of the social underdog, the Negro, in the fangs of unjust justice; idiocy is used rather in the way Faulkner uses it, as a symbol of futility, of the impossibility of redemption although, again, Benjy is given a more comprehensive meaning than

From *Jahrbuch für Amerikastudien* Band 8. © 1963 by Klaus Lubbers. Originally entitled "The Necessary Order: A Study of Theme and Structure in Carson McCullers's Fiction."

is Antonapoulos in *The Heart Is a Lonely Hunter*; finally, lust is transformed into a more complex theme that is central to her prose: it is the constant insistence on the impossibility of mutual love. All of these themes spread a web of sadness, isolation and disenchantment over Carson McCullers's work.

As she follows up the issues of Faulkner's earlier period, most of his later and more significant themes are lacking. She is far more concerned with the present than with the past, and therefore the collective burdens of fathers and forebears have but little weight on the outcome of her novels. In a sense, she entirely forgoes the broad social and historical dimensions that Faulkner and, for that matter, Robert Penn Warren are so keenly aware of. Moreover, she is out of touch with nature or, to put it in Faulkner's phrase, the land, in which he seems to have anchored some of his more recently voiced hope and affirmation. There is but little change of outlook in her development; the same ideas, though intensified and formally varied, are harped on repeatedly. Thirdly, in her attitude toward her themes and characters, she fails to develop Faulkner's passion and obsession; she remains cool and detached, at the most, compassionate. Wherever her heart goes into her pages, it tends to add pathetic touches that, at times, verge on the sentimental. Still, her "ordinary town," the setting of her plots, lies in the middle of the deep South and can be imagined in Georgia, the state in which she was born. Although she has lived in New York for the greater part of her life, in her novels she never strays beyond the boundaries of the Mason-Dixon line.

As the problems of themes and structure have so far presented the main difficulties in the scanty criticism devoted to her work, I propose to examine in chronological order the interrelation of themes and artistic organization in her five long prose pieces, omitting her few short stories as they are of little help in clarifying the subject carved out for discussion.

I

The most puzzling novel is undoubtedly *The Heart Is a Lonely Hunter*. Written when its author was only twenty-two, it met with wholesale condemnation as morbid on the one hand, with unlimited acclaim on the other. What has led to some confusion is the multiplicity of characters, parallel actions and understandings of "truth" (none of which seems central) without any apparent norm to give the plot perspective. As a consequence, the story gives the impression of being made up of loosely juxtaposed elements which are parts of a barely coherent whole. Unless one can perceive governing patterns, the book leaves in the reader a disjointed, if not chaotic, effect. Almost any of the main figures or "truths" might then be selected as central, summing up the total experience. One might, with Carpenter, find that the narrative ends on Mick Kelly's note of frustration; one might think the novel "intended to present an ironic parable of fascism"; one might even assume that it is altogether unintelligible. Even a recent study which has so far gone the longest way toward an exegesis of the book, denies it formal unity. It is therefore on formal links that we shall have to concentrate to grasp the relative importance of the major characters and their ideas. The author's technique of side-by-side action, of parallel movement, calls for a careful study of the ways in which characters and subplots are presented and brought to converge.

The story is mainly concerned with four figures grappling with life from the different angles of growing childhood, the race problem, socialism and common sense. In addition, there are a couple of deaf-mutes that are closely tied up with the meaning of the whole. The most obvious and effective device to throw into relief the personages of Biff, Mick, Jake and Copeland would seem to be the wheel image which elucidates both their isolation and their joint dependence upon Singer. After coming singly to see the mute for several months, they all happen to meet at his room one day halfway through the book. Although formerly each had had much to confide to the mute, it now turns out that they are incapable of communicating with each other: "Each person addressed his words mainly to the mute. Their thoughts seemed to converge in him as the spokes of a wheel lead to the center hub." The hub, however, is unable to fulfill its function. Singer himself is bewildered and does not understand the awkward situation. He can only devote himself to one at a time by listening patiently to his sorrows, but he cannot help four at once, nor can the others talk to him unless alone with him. As a result, after they are gone, he writes one of his desperate and longing letters to his imbecile friend in the mental institution. This letter, as the previous ones, is never mailed because the Greek is an illiterate. While the others lean on Singer, he in turn depends upon an idiot. There is an "ironic void" at the center of the human wheel, stressed by the fact that "Singer" is both deaf and mute: neither can he listen to people properly nor give adequate counsel. The irony is enhanced by Antonapoulos being not only a deaf-mute, but an illiterate idiot.

The meeting at Singer's apartment reveals the human predicament as seen by the author: any hope of understanding is illusory; there is no real center of gravity toward which men may flock for help. On the same night, Singer has a dream that corroborates how far he himself is from imagining his person in a middle position:

> There were dull yellow lanterns lighting up a dark flight of stone
> steps. Antonapoulos kneeled at the top of these steps. He was naked
> and he fumbled with something that he held above his head as though

in prayer. He himself knelt halfway down the steps. He was naked and cold and he could not take his eyes from Antonapoulos and the thing he held above him. Behind him on the ground he felt the one with the mustache and the girl and black man and the last one. They knelt naked and he felt their eyes upon him. And behind them there were uncounted crowds of kneeling people in the darkness. . . . Then suddenly there was a ferment. In the upheaval the steps collapsed and he felt himself falling downward.

(The "thing" that the Greek holds in his hands is later identified as his little brass cross.) This dream is Singer's view of the matter and rightly summarizes the experience of the foregone day: the others' eyes rest upon him while he gazes at his (Catholic) friend holding the crucifix. There had already been a specific undertone in the presentation of the characters through the wheel: that of people seeking for a private confessor, a redeemer—an idea which has further ramifications in the novel and that we will presently discuss. In an abortive way, Singer's vision is an unconscious, ironic rendering of the dream found in William Langland's edificatory poem: there the shepherd-poet sees Pierce and the truth-loving crowd, and Pierce eventually leads the pilgrims along the right way to the tower of truth. Singer's dream remodels the human relationships of the novel by establishing a personal hierarchy which, to be sure, is illusive and collapses in the very dream, thus foreshadowing the outcome of the book. Just as the others read qualities into Singer to which he cannot lay claim, the mute interprets the character of his friend according to his own needs. He thinks him "very subtle and wise" and later compares him to "some wise king from a legend."

The wheel image, then, together with the mute's vision, groups the persons in a way consistent not with actuality, but with an imagined and hoped-for order. The wheel, if it did exist, would give meaning to the lives of Biff, Mick, Jake and Copeland, but not to Singer's life. The mute, as we see in his dream vision, can only exist in a world in which he may look up to Antonapoulos. Thus the death of the one at the top will lead to the despair of the one next to him and will, in succession, cause changes in the lives of the four still further down. We have here a hierarchy based on misunderstandings, due to the empty space in the immediately higher rank. The configuration falls apart with only the idiot content, at peace with himself and the world because he alone has no need for human sympathy and communication.

Structurally, Singer as the hub seems to occupy the dominating position in the novel. It is his figure that gives the book its frame in the first section, it is his exit that closes its main portion and causes Copeland, Jake, Mick and Biff to revise their differing experiences with life, now life without the illusive prop.

However, there is a neatly elaborated structure running counter to this grouping. It arranges the characters in a different way, namely in proportion to the viability of their ideas. If we exclude Singer, the persons are introduced in the following order at the beginning: Biff dominates the second chapter, the third is mainly about Mick, the fourth is devoted to Jake, the fifth deals with Copeland. Although of necessity a host of others is brought on the scene—Alice, Copeland's children, Mick's numerous family—we perceive that from the beginning throughout the work each chapter is dedicated to one of the four characters. They live in their individual divisions as in watertight compartments. This technique of encasing the figures in their separate worlds underscores their isolation in life. each stands by himself. In the epilogue, the third section, the order of presentation is exactly reversed: Copeland is followed by Jake, Mick by Biff. Between the beginning and the end there is thus a chiastic correspondence in the order of presenting the figures. The intentional correspondence of the novel's first and last parts is furthermore made explicit by another device: each comprises the same time span of twenty-four hours while the main section spreads out over the period of a whole year (from August 1938 to July 1939). The four connected chapters of the first part (2–5) move from late Saturday to late Sunday in May 1938; the four chapters of the short concluding section cover the morning, afternoon, evening and night of August 21, 1939, ending in the small hours of the next morning. If we accept the different distribution of emphasis—different from the grouping according to the wheel image and Singer's vision quoted above—we see the figures in a new order of importance ranging from Biff through Mick and Jake down to Copeland.

It might at this point be noted that the tripartite overall structure is anticipated in the very first chapter. The sequence of introduction, life with a friend, loss of a friend and subsequent loneliness, that is here played out on Singer's level, recurs in a more complex form on the level of the other participants in the drama. What the Greek meant for the mute, the mute, successively, comes to mean for Biff, Mick, Jake and Copeland, so that the ultimate support lies in the imbecile. Singer's disillusionment is accomplished at the end of the first section in a similar manner as that of the others is at the end of the novel.

What does this sequence and this regrouping of the personages that both adds and runs counter to the flight-of-steps image tell us about the meaning of The Heart Is a Lonely Hunter? What are the grounds for this double grouping? The main theme of Carson McCullers's first novel is not the social problem nor is it primarily that of human isolation. It is rather the question of truth and illusion (or, disillusionment). Each of the four characters around Singer is in his own way concerned with distinguishing truth from illusion. Biff Brannon, the owner of the New York Café, a man "tough and small and common," looks out for truth behind appearances from behind his restaurant counter. He is a realist, interested in facts and the whys behind them. For the adolescent Mick Kelly, the problem of truth is that of initiation into a drab world. For a long time, she is unable to make her imaginary and her real worlds meet. Her friendly "inside room" is furnished with her dreams and aspirations while the "outside room" of the world leaves her puzzled and perplexed. For Jake Blount, the eternally roving Marxian revolutionary, the world is similarly split up: there are the "knows" and the "don't knows" according to people's reactions to his socialist good tidings. The fourth person is another gospeler, the Negro doctor Benedict Copeland, obsessed with the dissemination of "real truths." He has sacrificed his family life to the pursuit of his "real true purpose" of liberating his race. He is an atheist, suspicious of the heart, living only with his brain. To complicate matters, there is a fifth truth looming in the rear: the lesson that Biff's wife Alice selects for Sunday school, Christ's gathering of the disciples, together with the text "All men seek for Thee." This truth is constantly played off against the other 'truths.' It is developed and brought to focus by Biff as he ponders Singer's capacity of impersonal devotion to anyone who will talk to him:

> Why?
> Because in some men it is in them to give up everything personal at some time before it ferments and poisons—throw it to some human being or some human idea. They have to. In some men it is in them —The text is 'all men seek for Thee.' Maybe that was why— maybe—.

With this old and central truth all of the four characters are confronted: Biff through Alice, Mick through the Negro servant Portia, Jake through Simms, the frantic street preacher, Copeland through his father-in-law and again through his daughter Portia, and Singer through the primitive religiosity of his feebleminded friend who, after all, is a man of prayer. The reaction of all, with shadings, is negative. They live by their own truths and it is important to consider what becomes of them in the last section.

The first we encounter in the morning of August 21 after Singer's suicide is Copeland. His work has failed, his sacrifice has been in vain; he moves out of the town "exhausted and sick in spirit." The second to appear is Jake. Also his task has collapsed incomplete, symbolized by a general fight at the carnival show where he had worked as a mechanic. "He remembered all the innermost thoughts he had told to Singer, and with his death it seemed that they were lost." Characteristically, neither of the reformers has a "home," the Negro being estranged from his family through lack of feeling, the socialist being a stray pebble throughout the book. Yet there is a difference between the two: the doctor takes his departure to die, whereas Jake's exodus will lead him onward to the next station on his way as "a stranger in a strange land." Like most of the other figures, he defines his ultimate position in a dream which had haunted him many times and which he is only now able to recollect clearly. In a vision of himself, walking among a crowd of people in an eastern town, he carries a huge covered basket, "not knowing where to lay down the burden he had carried in his arms so long." There is no change, no arrival, no resting place for this nomad; he moves along a line that by chance had led him into the town and will necessarily lead him out of it after his failure.

With Singer gone, Mick also evaluates her youth, now suspended between her former dreams and plans and the grown-up world whose motto is neatly summarized by the Woolworth maxim for the salesgirls, "Keep on your toes and smile." Her life has reached a turning point. "It was like she was shut out from the inside room." Plays and the excitements of youth have given way to work and tiredness. But beside the drudgery to which she has to yield too early, she hopes that her inside room has been some good, has had some reason. Her change consists in crossing over to the outside room without giving up the place in which she had lived for years. In her there is acceptance of reality alongside youthful idealism.

Like Mick, Biff also stays in town, and in the last chapter, which is his, place and time take on symbolic significance. The historical time in the course of the novel's development has moved up to point of intense crisis. It stops a few days before the outbreak of the Second World War, the great political events being thus paralleled to the happenings in the lives of our characters. Furthermore, time in the last chapter extends from shortly before midnight to the early hours of a new day, i.e., across a threshold to a point of great stillness, realization and awakening. His café is the only store on the street with an open door at night. Biff wants to meet all people, also those that will only come at this time. Now that Alice is dead, his idea of love has changed; his personal loves are forgotten, and he has come close to Singer's alleged sympathy with all men. In the loneliness of the empty night he tries to reason out "the puzzle of Singer and the rest of them." Suddenly, as he stands "transfixed, lost in his meditations," he has a vision of it all:

> For in a swift radiance of illumination, he saw a glimpse of human struggle and of valor. Of the endless fluid passage of humanity through endless time. And of those who labor and of those who — one word — love. . . . Between the two worlds he was suspended. He saw that he was looking at his own face in the counter glass before him. . . . The left eye delved narrowly into the past while the right

gazed wide and affrighted into a future of blackness, error, and ruin.
And he was suspended between radiance and darkness. Between bitter irony and faith. Sharply he turned away.

Here Biff, who had long ago rejected church and religion, takes up Singer's
burden of impersonal love, but he does more than the mute. He judges life
soberly, perceiving its contrasting aspects. He is ready to wait, to endure dog-
gedly though the prospects are gloomy.

Let us come back to the biblical implications of *The Heart Is a Lonely
Hunter*. They can be stated in terms of a general need among men for a confessor, a mediator between them and God. This need is expressed through the
wheel image (from the narrator's point of view) and the subsequent flight-of-
steps vision (from Singer's point of view). It is also apparent in Alice's Sunday
school text. In addition, there is Simm's chalk message inviting people to listen
to his sermon: "He Died to Save You. Hear the Story of His Love and Grace." It
is true that men are searching for meaning, but they are skeptical and run past
the written message. The Bible only reminds Biff of his youth. Jake had even
been an ardent believer in Christ during his boyhood. He had gone so far as to
nail down his hand to the table, with the stigma still visible; but that is all. The
Christian doctrine has no longer any force on the lives of the characters, except
the Negroes. Because they discard it, they have to substitute other truths, and
since these prove more or less private ones that cannot be shared or spread out,
communication is obstructed. We see each of the four figures strive by themselves,
elevating Singer to the status of a vicarious savior, a mute monument of their
own condition. The two socialists try to convert others to their beliefs; Mick and
Biff are coming to terms with their own confusing worlds without inviting fol-
lowers. As in *The Sound and the Fury*, the Christian image provides a frame
which is not filled out. At the crisis in Singer's room, it functions ironically, and
at the end it is rudely dispensed with in the scene where Jake makes fun of
Simms. The meaning which the book finally adds up to is this: Christ's gospel is
dead for the protagonists. The substituted truths they embrace are private truths,
not comprehensive enough to include others. The most acceptable truth is Biff's
(which, by the way, comes closest to the biblical doctrine). It is Christ's message
of love in a secular form which Brannon has arrived at by constantly attempting
to solve the riddle of Singer's life, the hard path toward unrequited human sympathy in an exacting world heading into darkness.

II

As the structure of the novel conveys meaning and helps elucidate the theme,
its shortcomings, as is the case in Carson McCullers's second book, affect both
theme and meaning in a deplorable way. *Reflections in a Golden Eye* was, on its

appearance, generally considered as a proof that its author's preoccupation had become fixed on abnormality, on the "freakish." It is, indeed, a work almost as quizzical as its predecessor. The veil that surrounds the last scene can never quite be lifted. Even such a stout defender of her art as Oliver Evans does not give it more than passing attention. Later in his essay, however, he remarks that the closed pattern of spiritual isolation can be tracked through all of Mrs. McCullers's novels. Tennessee Williams, in his 1950 introduction to the novelette, comments: "There is an absolute mastery of design. There is a lapidary precision about the structure of this second book." Despite these assertions, it can hardly be called as successful as *The Heart Is a Lonely Hunter*.

In a simpler form, stripped of the ironic hierarchy of truth seekers and of the racial and social involvements, the old theme of the impossibility of reciprocal love — apparent in the relations of Mick and Biff, Singer and Antonapoulos — is narrowed down to one-sided love between the sexes and presented in a singular constellation of characters. In a prewar southern army camp, Captain Weldon Penderton is at the same time repelled and fascinated by young Private Ellgee Williams, whom he shoots on the last page for sneaking into his wife's room at night to watch her sleeping. Leonora Penderton, alienated from her husband, carries on a love affair with her neighbor, Major Morris Langdon. Mrs. Alison Langdon's sole consolation is her friendship with the old unsuccessful Lieutenant Weincheck and the unrestricted devotion of her Filipino servant Anacleto.

The novel gains its shape only from the relation of the personages to one another. As the marital lives of the Pendertons and the Langdons are a failure from the outset, there remains as the most vital and normal human bond the mutual attachment of Leonora and Morris, leaving Penderton and Alison dangling at the loose ends of the chain. Yet, as the first novel has already revealed, man is in urgent need of an object for his emotions, however odd and deviating it may seem from what is considered normal:

> There are times when a man's greatest need is to have someone to
> love, some focal point for his diffused emotions. Also there are times
> when the irritations, disappointments, and fears of life, restless as
> spermatozoids, must be released in hate.

For the captain, who has never known real love, release is found in hating Private Williams with an intensity which becomes obsessive. For the major's unloved, sick and suffering wife, her servant figures as a confidant of her plans for divorce and escape. Into this emotional equilibrium Williams enters as a blind force. In his unthinking, trancelike way, he indirectly causes Alison to be committed to a sanatorium in which she soon dies; moreover, he precipitates his own destruction.

The persons are judged and thus given perspective from the two points of view of Penderton and Alison. One night after a party in the third chapter, Alison sums up her impressions of the others:

> Everyone she had known in the past five years was somehow wrong
> —that is, everyone except Weincheck and of course Anacleto and
> little Catherine. Morris Langdon in his blunt way was as stupid and
> as heartless as a man could be. Leonora was nothing but an animal.
> And thieving Weldon Penderton was at bottom hopelessly corrupt.
> What a gang. Even she herself she loathed.

Of all the characters, she is the only one who takes note of and evaluates her surroundings; whereas the captain is exclusively concerned with his own strange situation. In an illuminating passage toward the close he discusses his plight with Langdon:

> "You mean that any fulfillment obtained at the expense of normalcy
> is wrong, and should not be allowed to bring happiness. In short, it
> is better, because it is morally honorable, for the square peg to keep
> scraping about the round hole rather than to discover and use the
> unorthodox square that would fit it"?
> "Why, you put it exactly right," the Major said. "Don't you agree
> with me?" "No," said the Captain. . . . With gruesome vividness the
> Captain suddenly looked into his soul and saw himself . . . there
> came to him a distorted doll-like image, mean of countenance and
> grotesque in form.

A further frame of reference for the figures concerned is provided by the setting and the unwieldy horse Firebird. "The horse may stand as an embodiment of instincts and the military camp as an image of social regimentation. Between these two, men must somehow mediate." At the far end of the primitive side stands Williams, akin in his sun worship to Juliet of D. H. Lawrence's short story "Sun." He lives in complete harmony with crude, instinctual life, more so than Eleonora and Langdon, all of whom are significantly able to handle Firebird. On the other side we could place Penderton who in his mad gallop with the thoroughbred experiences the rapture and total abandonment to sheer life at least at one time in his coward existence, thereby ruining the animal. Langdon figures somewhere in the middle. He functions best between the two poles, as is indicated in his maxim: "Only two things matter to me now—to be a good animal and to serve my country. A healthy body and patriotism."

The *novella* is composed of four parts which all close with the private watching Eleonora. Moreover, the first two begin with Williams. Thus the narrative circles around to his uncanny visits at each juncture. Nevertheless, in terms of organization, a more central character is Alison. Her death forms the watershed movement of the plot. It leaves the major suddenly helpless; his thoughts now gather entirely on his dead wife and his life with her in the past. Also the captain experiences a change: "To him it seemed that not only had Alison died, but that in some mysterious way the lives of all three of them had come to a close." He becomes absorbed in his hate of the soldier, and his murder upsets all relationships.

Reflections in a Golden Eye can best be regarded as a repeated but abortive attempt to deal anew with a concatenation of bizarre feelings. The question of truth is dropped, and the rendering of strange emotions left without a final comment. The main defect is a structural one. It lies in the absence of the necessary observer, a Nick Carraway, to give meaning to the last act of the tragedy which the form does not make clear as in *The Heart Is a Lonely Hunter*. The author, obviously aware of this failure, was later to make amends in *The Ballad of the Sad Café*.

III

Everybody seemed to belong to some special bunch . . . she wasn't a member of any bunch.

She belonged to no club and was a member of nothing in the world.

If we read these two statements out of their contexts, we would probably be surprised to discover that the first is made about Mick Kelly, the second about Frankie Addams, her fictional successor, on the opening page of *The Member of the Wedding*. Formally as well as thematically, the natural sequel of Mrs. McCullers's first book is not the laconic fable of 1941, but her third work which by some critics has been called her greatest achievement to date. Down to details, it is firmly rooted in the Mick Kelly portion of the first work. Apart from the heroine, Portia and Bubber recur as Berenice and John Henry—with only the "bad" little brother changed into an angel cousin. Also minor figures are encountered for the second time: Highboy is brought back to life as T. T. Williams, William has turned Honey, both of the latter running into trouble with the law. The author has fastened her attention on the adolescent's fate and developed it by itself. The book is therefore easier to read and needs less explanation. The multi-level structure of *The Heart Is a Lonely Hunter* and the emotional intricacy of *Reflections in a Golden Eye* have yielded to simpler organization, the constantly shifting focus now resting on one character.

The story is exclusively that of the protagonist, the aimlessly roaming girl who, on the occasion of her brother's marriage, strikes upon the tragicomic idea of becoming a "member of the wedding" and of forever living together with the couple. As this is impossible, disappointment is the inevitable consequence. But out of her despair Frankie (who is one year younger than the initiated Mick Kelly) finds her way back to the illusions of youth. This material is arranged according to a threefold principle of composition: the distribution of the action on mainly three days corresponds with the division of the novel into three parts, of which the middle part is in turn broken up into three chapters moving through the three times—morning, afternoon and evening—of a single day. In addition there are the three main figures and the three names the protagonist assumes on her three stages of coming to grips with herself and the world.

The most revealing part of the book is its middle section. After Frankie's sudden realization at the end of the opening division—"at last she knew just who she was and understood where she was going"—we follow F. Jasmine through her exuberant activity on the day before the marriage: her morning walk through the town (II, 1), her long afternoon talk with Berenice and John Henry in the kitchen (II, 2), and her frustrating evening adventure with the soldier she had met in the morning (II, 3). In the tectonic structure of the novel, II, 2 occupies the exact middle position. Climax as well as ultimate failure are indicated in the image of its first sentence: "The afternoon was like the center of the cake that Berenice had baked last Monday, a cake which failed." In their talk about love, the Negro servant tells the girl the story of her past three marriages as a warning, but it is evident that both are at cross-purposes. F. Jasmine continues her ravings about her new sense of "connection" and envisions herself and the couple as touring the world and making "thousands and thousands and thousands of friends." This "urge to merge" is an escape from her own self. Frankie dreams of getting away from her stagnant existence, of going to Alaska and joining the Esquimeaux, and at the end she actually tries to leave the town at night. Her wishes to escape and to belong, of course, do not lead her anywhere. In order to see life as it is, she would have to face her own image as Biff Brannon does. But to do this she is still too young. For this reason, she is also unable to perceive the truth behind Berenice's words following her own outburst. To Berenice, life is like a spider's web in which man is caught:

> "We all of us somehow caught. We born this way or that way and
> we don't know why. But we caught anyhow. I born Berenice. You
> born Frankie. John Henry born John Henry. And maybe we wants
> to widen and bust free. But no matter what we do we still caught.
> Me is me and you is you and he is he. We each of us somehow
> caught all by ourself."

In her tragic realization and acceptance of life, Berenice reminds us not only of Portia and Brannon, but also of Faulkner's Dilsey and her quality of endurance. She is experienced in life, realistic, and forms the one polar end of the three with the innocent John Henry on the other side and F. Jasmine in the middle. This interrelation is symbolized in the way they usually sing: "The old Frankie sang up and down the middle space between John Henry and Berenice, so that their three voices were joined, and the parts of the song were woven together." The long scene ends without F. Jasmine having profited from the conversation. She is yet unfinished, like the tune that Mr. Schwarzenbaum, the piano tuner, plays in the neighborhood, a tune ringing solemnly and insistently into the kitchen. All through the afternoon, he plays up and down the scale, sticking at the seventh note and not finishing the gamut. The difference between the instrument, at last adjusted, and the still discordant girl becomes obvious. She has yet to go through the jarring experience with the soldier, the wedding and the unsuccessful escape before she is able to recover her youthful strength and buoyancy.

The novel, less ambitious than its predecessors, shows a formal control in which stagnation and action are well balanced. Avoiding the complexity of relationships, it concentrates on a main character who is freakish, to be sure, like the other protagonists, but who is counterpoised by a norm that gives it perspective and significance.

IV

There is a rhythm in Carson McCullers's output: full-length treatment alternates with the short novel or *novelette*, a form in which her problems of love and isolation can be stated more cogently. The choice of the intermediary fictional genre seems especially adequate as it allows of condensation of atmosphere and detachment of the narrator. *The Ballad of the Sad Café* marks the artistic climax of her writing up to that time. It contains a philosophy of love that has slowly evolved through her earlier works and has now reached a point of completeness where it is not only presented dramatically, but also explicitly in a reflective passage: not only may love not be returned by the beloved, it may also cause the latter to hate the lover. This idea is the result of a consistent development of such relations as between the deaf-mutes, and it accounts for the singular and terrible connection of the characters in her fourth book.

There is the handsome, evil Marvin Macy who falls in love with, and marries, Miss Amelia, a cross-eyed, masculine giantess in overalls. Amelia, however, despises his love and turns him off her premises. Whatever emotions she is capable of, she bestows on the unlovable hunchback Lymon Willis. The dwarf, for his part, spites his lover and craves for Marvin's affection when he returns from a term in the penitentiary to wreak his vengeance on Amelia. His love remains as unrequited as Amelia's love for him—three people on a chain with one end of it in deadly and unforgivable enmity with the other after the failure of the first love; one-sided love in recoil, working its own destruction. The theme apparent in the earlier novels is not changed but sharpened and given a more dramatic turn which involves more, and more violent, action.

Formally, the tale falls into three parts of equal length: there is (1) the arrival of the hunchback, his unexpectedly kind reception by Amelia, the town's rumors about the odd couple, and the transformation of Amelia's store into a café; (2) a middle section dealing with the growth of the café, the nature of love and, in retrospect, with Amelia's grotesque marriage; (3) the return of Marvin Macy, the hunchback's attachment to him, the increasing tension between the antagonists and the climactic wrestling match between Amelia and Marvin. These divisions are carefully balanced and connected with each other; the opening scene lays the cornerstone in Amelia's invitation to Lymon to stay with her. It stands out in striking contrast to the first scene of the last part where Marvin arrives and trespasses on the property. In both cases there follows a period of expectancy and rumors. In the first part, the town is left puzzled and talkative by the strange hospitality; in the final section, the time is filled with rising curiosity of the observers as to the outcome of the fight that is sensed by everyone. The third part of the introductory portion, again a scene, describes the hunchback's appearance in the store on the second day after his arrival, and its sudden change into a place of hospitality. This links up with the fighting between Amelia and Marvin in which the latter, by the dwarf's help at the critical moment, stays victorious, destroys the café and leaves the town with Lymon.

All the major happenings are thus concentrated in four scenes. They are watched by the townspeople who stand on the periphery as judges and witnesses. They play the part that in *Reflections in a Golden Eye* is inadequately filled out by Alison, leaving the earlier novelette without the necessary norm. Usually seen as a group or crowd—"think of them as a whole"—the people are sometimes divided into the malignant ones, "a few sensible men" and "the good people." Their presence, in retrospect, underscores the importance of Biff Brannon's interpreting role and gives added significance to Berenice's judgment of Frankie's youthful phantasies. The factory workers on Amelia's porch immediately feel "there was something wrong" in her behavior toward the dwarf. The same quality of alertness was visible in Biff: "The puzzle had taken root in him. It worried him in the back of his mind and left him uneasy. There was something wrong." We also remember the critical attitude that distinguished Alison among the "square pegs" of the human tangle in which she herself is partly involved: "Everyone she had known in the past five years was somehow wrong."

The role of objectification assigned to the outside figures by the author is moreover emphasized by another means: whenever one of the townspeople is characterized, the past-tense flow of the narrative is for a moment interrupted and the figure lifted into the light of a timeless present:

> Henry Macy . . . left the bottom step and disappeared. He *is* a good soul, and the hunchback's situation touched his heart.

> This is what happened to Marvin Macy, who *is* the opposite to his brother.

> The rumor was started by a weaver called Merlie Ryan. He *is* a man of not much account.

> Therefore, according to Mrs. McPhail, . . . who *is* continually moving her sticks of furniture . . . , these two were living in sin.

As is also elucidated by the last quotation, the outside world passes moral judgment on the protagonists. This is another way of objectification, although the narrator makes it clear that Miss Amelia cannot be judged by normal moral standards, just as Penderton assumes for himself the right of foregoing moral normalcy and living by his "square peg" standards.

A further device to introduce a critical plane are the reflective asides and the frequent addresses to the reader which establish a feeling of intimacy between him and the narrator. The most significant of these addresses is a strong allusion to the outcome of the book, connecting the uneventful middle section with the showdown on the last day: "So do not forget this Marvin Macy, as he is to act a terrible part in the story which is yet to come."

The handling of place contributes to the unity of the novelette. Already in *The Heart Is a Lonely Hunter* the strategy was discernible in the microcosm of Biff's restaurant with Singer sitting at a table in the middle of the room and Jake and Mick gravitating toward him. In fact, that scene, in the second chapter of the main section, contains in a nutshell the dramatic character arrangement of the whole novel. The "center" as the focal point of happenings also figures large in the "ballad." Not only does Amelia's building occupy the very middle of the town, but we also have a sense of finality when into that forbidding center the hunchback steps, making by his sprightly behavior the place of business transactions a "warm center point of the town" and gaining domination over Amelia. Later Marvin Macy, in his turn, lays claim to the spot, and "alone in the cleared center of the bright café" the wrestlers take their stand.

The book's title suggests an affinity with an old poetic genre. The novelette does, indeed, show characteristics of the ballad. There is the same brevity and dramatic intensity with which the fateful story is commemorated, an encounter that at one time affected the whole town community, and there is varied repetition that comes as a burden at caesurae in the narrative:

That was the way Marvin Macy came back from the penitentiary.

That is the way Marvin Macy crowded into Amelia's house.

That was how Miss Amelia was left alone in the town.

The most powerful effect radiates from the prologue which conjures up the absolute rottenness, stagnation and gloom of the present town, and alights on Amelia's old house, now boarded up, out of which "a face like the terrible dim faces known in dreams" will sometimes look down. It sets the mood for the tale now long passed and once more put before the reader's eye. The epilogue returns to the same atmosphere of dreariness and boredom. Yet there is something that is alive near the town, the chain gang made up of "twelve mortal men." In their song, both somber and joyful, which rouses ecstasy and fright in the listener, we hear the music of mankind imprisoned in its suffering, working and enduring, comparable to the final vision of Biff, but more hopeful of man's indestructibility.

V

It is a long way from Carson McCullers's first to her latest novel, written with her age in the meantime doubled and with tragic experience behind her. Although the old watermarks still show through the pages—loneliness, freakishness, men in pursuit of separate and clashing dreams, the odd, ironic human chain with the beloved lashing out at the lover—, her writing has apparently entered a new phase. Life has become more wholesome, order and meaning are perceived in it at last, and even mutual love begins to blossom.

The plot of *Clock Without Hands* is composed of four strands of action. Of the four characters that "move to their accomplished destiny through Sherman Pew," as the dust jacket blurb has it, J. T. Malone has the honor of opening and closing the book. His part begins as the saddest of all as he has to face the fact that he will die of leukemia. As we follow him through the fifteen months of his dying, we see him first unable to confront the reality of approaching death. He tries to find solace first in the delusion that his disease does not really exist, then in the comforting words of his friend, the old Judge, and finally in religion—but all in vain. It is only when he chances upon the idea that the greatest danger is that of losing one's self that he awakens to a sense of what life really means: that it is composed of the countless little miracles which man passes unnoticed. When with the beginning of a new season his last hour has come, he is no longer "a man watching a clock without hands." He rediscovers his long extinguished love for his wife and peaceably resigns himself to his premature end.

Malone, the pharmacist, is set off by contrast through Fox Clane, the Judge, a lumbering septuagenarian seemingly endowed with immortality itself. Wrapped up in his former greatness as a congressman, he will not admit to himself that he is guilty of his son's suicide resulting from their different conceptions of justice concerning the Negro. With him, for the first time, the southern past with its rhetoric, gyneolatry and segregation mania enters. But it is a dead past. Clane is unaware of the changed present. He is still obsessed with the dream of redeeming the Confederate money, an idea to which he wants to win over his grandson Jester as well as his Negro amanuensis Sherman Pew. Yet both lose faith in him, and he is left by Sherman, in whom he had put all his confidence, and even by Verily, his colored cook. His downfall comes when he tries to protest against the Supreme Court decision for school integration. The very passion with which he had fought all his life to preserve the old order plays a trick on him before the radio microphone. Unable to find the right words, he recites the Gettysburg address and is cut off.

In Jester Clane, the adolescent, we once again witness the struggles of initiation. He is trying to lift the veil from his father's mysterious death. When he learns that Johnnie Clane had taken his life after an unsuccessful attempt to rescue a Negro's life in court, he embraces his father's ideal of justice. Sherman Pew, the pathetic figure of a young colored orphan, striking out at Jester whenever the latter seeks his friendship and at the same time craving his affection, is in search of his mother. When he finds out that she was a white hussy and that his father was sentenced to death through the Judge's agency, his admiration for Clane turns to hate. Leaving him, he moves into the white section of the town and dies in a bombing in which the Judge, again, was instrumental.

The severe charges made by a reviewer—that the book "tends to be extremely fragile in structure" and that it is "so poorly constructed . . . that the symbolic scheme fails to carry strength or conviction"—cannot be maintained upon close reading. The four stories are integrated in various ways. There is first of all the vicious circle of love already found in *The Ballad of the Sad Café* with Sherman hating Jester and Jester venting his anger on his grandfather. There is, moreover, the double grouping of the boys in quest of truth about their parents in order to find a direction in their own lives, and of the friends, Malone and Clane, who are bound together by the shared problem of "livingness." Sherman's discovery of his father's execution sets him on a train of action "to do something, do something, do something," leading to his infringement of zoning laws and his death. For Jester, the questions "Who am I? What am I? Where am I going?" are answered at about the same time when he gathers that his father had died for the idea of equal justice: "having found his father he was able to find himself. He was his father's son and he was going to be a lawyer."

More central to the theme are the discoveries about life made by the other two. The Judge, despite his ravings about the feudal past, is a man living in the here and now. In a conversation with Sherman where he, in his usual grandiloquence, compares himself to the geniuses of history, he states:

> "I'd rather be Fox Clane than all the great and famous people. Can't you guess why?"
> This time Sherman looked at him.
> "Because I'm alive. And when you consider the trillions and trillions of dead people you realize what a privilege it is to be alive."

The Judge, a born hedonist, understands the little miracles—of dawn, moon, stars, shortcake and liquor—, he knows how to trick death with which he had had a skirmish. This quality of "livingness," as Carson McCullers calls it, is to be held against Malone's sense of having lost his life unnoticed piece by piece; he "thought of all the life he had spent unlived. He wondered how he could die since he had not yet lived." The experience (comparable to the last act of *Our Town* where Emily, returning from the dead, has a similar insight) is summed up by Clane in the paradoxical statement: "if I hadn't gone through the shadow of death I might never have seen the light." In this way, the old man comes to serve as a foil for Malone. The pharmacist, in the course of his dying, slowly outgrows his initial conviction that there is in the world "no order or conceivable design" and arrives at his final realization on his deathbed: "in dying, living assumed order and a simplicity that Malone had never before known."

VI

Order is the keynote of *Clock Without Hands*. It is the order of the heart that, even if sometimes crazy and often complex, gives peace and serenity to the protagonist's end of life. Looking back over the themes of Carson McCullers's books, one perceives a gradual development from the physically and psychologically outré to the normal, from the freakish to the wholesome, from frustration and defeat to acceptance with the insistence upon man's responsibility, from chaos to order. Her first novels still fall under the observation made by Kenneth Burke about the state of literary affairs in the early forties:

> The great political confusion of the present which is matched in the poetic sphere by a profusion of rebirth rituals, with a great rise of

adolescent characters as the bearers of "representative rôles" (adolescence being the transitional stage *par excellence*), gives reason to believe that we are in a kind of "neo-evangelical" era, struggling to announce a new conception of purpose.

Both the latter-day evangelists and the adolescents are important figures in her first and third books and their ideas have to be reduced to proper proportions by means of structural devices and contrasting characters. Thus, order in *The Heart Is a Lonely Hunter* is mainly imposed by the principle of organization, as we have seen, and by the central role which Biff Brannon plays. His importance, however, still depends on the place he is given within the *formal* framework of the novel. In *Reflections in a Golden Eye*, the theme of one-sided love is tentatively developed and brought to an unsatisfactory conclusion. The antithesis of the double ethical norm—"square peg" standard versus the feeble judgment passed by Alison as a moral arbiter—is not resolved and leaves the three surviving personages in an unexplained chaos. By a shift in emphasis, reduction of characters and concentration on one major theme, a balanced world emerges at the end of *The Member of the Wedding*. Here, for the last time, the adolescent is allowed a dominating part. This novel as well as the army camp novelette are variations on themes inherent in portions of the first book whereas *The Ballad of the Sad Café* belongs to a new category in matter and manner. The theme of love chasing its tail forms the logical capstone of an evolution through the three previous works. Its morbidity is made bearable and convincing by narrative detachment, remoteness in time and the witnessing town that stays outside the emotional boundary line. With *Clock Without Hands* a new concept of order is announced. Life becomes a state in which, at least at the end, everything is in its right place.

The overall theme of Carson McCullers's books is that of man's problematic and painful existence with various veerings from its proper course. Man's drab life is presented at critical points such as adolescence, loss of friendship, oncoming death, and leads to types of escape, imaginary and real. Escape may be actual as in Frankie's case; but it is of short duration and fails due to lack of direction. In its extreme form, it becomes the negation of meaning in life itself, as in Singer's suicide. Another source of escape is the recourse to the "inner room." Fancy fastens on the distant in time and place; the seashell on Frankie's desk stands for the warm wash of the Gulf of Mexico, her glass snow globe reminds her of cool Alaska, the wedding proves more attractive because it takes place in "Winter" Hill. Uneventful life is also adorned by lying which provides a form of vicarious life. Yet inevitably, man is brought back from fanciful flights. Without fail his wishful dreams are thwarted by the onslaughts of reality and only his nightmares materialize. His experience is that of being caught, of being left as an alien in a strange land, symbolized in the corresponding images of the prisoner caged in a stone cell with iron bars before the windows and of the chain that both connects and isolates the members of the gang. The song of the "twelve mortal men" mediates between the tragic vision of Biff and the rediscovered little miracles of everyday life that reconcile J. T. Malone with his too early death. His love for his wife has returned just as Martin Meadows in a short story "A Domestic Dilemma" finds back to "the immense complexity of love." Thus the burden of impersonal love that Biff takes up and that is rationalized in an early story "A Tree. A Rock. A Cloud" is replaced by mutual personal love for the first time.

The imaginary scope of the author is not wide. Typical figures and ideas, characteristic scenes, and forms of behavior recur in all of her books. Nor does her fictional town alter much. It is expanded or contracted as needed, a café or a drugstore forms its significant center: in short, the stage remains, the properties are shifted. On the stage, man's drama is enacted, and it is his attitude toward life that has undergone a change and testifies that, in the second decade of her writing, Mrs. McCullers's themes have changed, tending to emphasize the one side of Brannon's vision, putting more stress on "radiance" and "faith" than upon "irony" and "darkness."

LAWRENCE GRAVER

Penumbral Insistence:
McCullers's Early Novels

Any reader who wishes to determine the characteristic strengths and limitations of Carson McCullers as a writer could do no better than to begin with *The Heart Is a Lonely Hunter*. Not only is this first novel an admirably complete introduction to her themes and subject matter, but it raises in a complex and provocative way the major critical issues posed by all her important work. The scene is the deep South; the characters are estranged and disadvantaged; and the theme is loneliness and the inevitable frustrations of love.

When the book opens, John Singer and Spiros Antonapoulos, two deaf-mutes, have been joined for ten years in a close but enigmatic friendship. The active and quick-witted Singer has been entirely infatuated with his impassive and feebleminded friend. Although most of the other people in this depressed factory town are isolated, the two mutes never seem lonely at all. Singer gives; his friend receives; and each seems absorbed in his role as lover and beloved. But suddenly Antonapoulos becomes mysteriously ill and a social menace, stealing silverware, jostling strangers, urinating in public places. Despite his distress and passionate concern, Singer can do nothing; the deranged Greek is packed off to an asylum two hundred miles away. At this point, still very early in the story, Singer involuntarily enters the life of the community by renting a room in the Kelly house and taking his meals at the New York Café.

During the course of the next few months, Singer unwittingly becomes the focal point of the lives of four other people, who, visiting his room, see in him a mysterious figure to complete their own obsessive but fragmentary dreams. For

From *Seven American Women Writers of the Twentieth Century: An Introduction.* © 1963, 1964, 1966, 1968, 1969, 1977 by the University of Minnesota. The University of Minnesota Press, 1977.

Mick Kelly, a twelve-year-old tomboy with a blossoming gift for music, Singer's imagined harmony of spirit brings Mozart to mind. To the crusading Negro doctor Benedict Copeland, the mute symbolizes an all-too-rare instance of white compassion. For Jake Blount, a haggard radical agitator with a greater gift for talk than action, Singer is divine because he listens. For Biff Brannon, the café owner who self-consciously observes the human pageant, Singer is a fit subject for contemplation because of the attention paid to him by others. None of these dreamers knows of Singer's love for Antonapoulos; nor are they aware of the bewilderment with which he observes their interest in him. When Antonapoulos dies, Singer commits suicide, and the disciples are left to ponder and to grieve.

From the opening pages of *The Heart Is a Lonely Hunter* one is aware that this strange and absorbing story is designed to be read both as a realistic tale of a half-dozen displaced southerners and as a generalized parable on the nature of human illusion and love. And, at the start at least, each level operates satisfactorily with the other. All the carefully observed details needed to authenticate the mutes are present. Antonapoulos, fat and slovenly, works in a fruit store; Singer, tall and immaculately dressed, engraves silver for a local jeweler. Their routine is carefully set, odd perhaps in its regularity, but entirely credible: they play at chess, and go once a week to the library, to the movies, and to a local photography store. As we move on, characters read *Popular Mechanics* and write letters to Jeanette MacDonald; they sing "Love's Old Sweet Song" and "K-K-K-Katie," smoke Target tobacco and speak of Joe Louis and Man Mountain Dean. Behind the exotic Georgian passion play stand Chamberlain, Munich, and the Danzig Corridor, and when Mrs. McCullers stops to describe a character from the viewpoint of Biff Brannon, she writes with the specificity familiar in traditional realistic fiction.

Yet along with the virtues of specification go the vaguer promptings of allegory. The symmetrical obsessions of Singer's four admirers quickly make him a special case, more interesting as a catalyst than as a complex human being; and soon afterwards the admirers themselves take on generalized significance: the adolescent, the idealistic Negro, the failed reformer, the philosophical student of human affairs. Through the passion with which each constructs the god he needs, he bears ironical witness to the many and wayward forms of human mythmaking.

For the first one hundred pages of *The Heart Is a Lonely Hunter*, Mrs. McCullers is able to persuade us that contemporary reality and legendary story are one; but soon afterwards her technique falters and the novel becomes increasingly unsatisfactory both as document and as myth. On the literal level the difficulties center on implausible psychology and faulty observation of character. Biff Brannon is introduced as a man with a rare gift for disinterested observation and described in such a way as to suggest that he should function as Mrs. McCullers's *raisonneur*, the one person to make objective sense of the action. As a café owner, he can see more of the drama than anyone else and he is sympathetic to a wide range of emotional grotesques; as a male with a strong feminine strain, he is able to temper the chill of analysis with the warmth of an intuitive compassion. Following the presentation of Singer, Biff is the first of the main characters to be introduced, and his reflections form the coda that brings the novel to an end.

Throughout the early pages, Biff is described as thoughtful, inquisitive, and alert; whenever something happens, he is often the first, perhaps the only, person to notice. As the pattern of the action evolves, however, Biff is of little use beyond his ability to tell us things we have already established on our own. Sometimes, his vaunted insight is merely banal: "By nature all people are of both sexes. So that marriage and the bed is not all by any means. The proof? Real youth and old age. Because often old men's voices grow high and reedy and they take on a mincing walk." But most often his discoveries are posed in terms of coils, puzzles, unanswered questions; after rubbing his nose, narrowing his eyes, fixing his stare, he is most likely to come up with this: "How Singer had been before was not important. The thing that mattered was the way Blount and Mick made of him a sort of homemade God. Owing to the fact he was a mute they were able to give him all the qualities they wanted him to have. Yes. But how could such a strange thing come about? And why?"

It is just "how it came about" and "why" that Biff is never able to tell us, and—on many of the more important matters—neither can Mrs. McCullers. In this respect, the fundamental weakness of *The Heart Is a Lonely Hunter* is that past midpoint, the central theme (men make strange gods in their own image) is not so much developed as embroidered by still another fancy but no more enlightening illustration.

Related to this inadequacy is Mrs. McCullers's failure to establish a satisfactory relationship between the various idealizations of Singer and what actually happens to each dreamer in the novel. A number of commentators have insisted that the forlorn fate of each character at the end of the book is prompted by Singer's suicide. When the Kelly family is pressed by poverty, Mick quits school to work in the dime store, her musical promise thwarted. Copeland, devastated by the bestial white torture of his prisoner son, goes in broken health to live with relatives who ignore his message. But these events are not causally related to Singer's death. The Kelly family is impoverished because of damages they must pay to the mother of a child their son injured, and Mick took the dime store job while Singer was still alive; in fact, he approved the choice. Copeland is shattered not by anything related to Singer, but by impotence, frozen incomprehension, and the obvious failure of his dream.

There is a growing sense, toward the close of the novel, that the death of God is anticlimactic, or perhaps even beside the point. The dreamers would have been doomed to frustration had the mute never lived, and the kind of fierce inevitability that so beautifully links a Kurtz to a Marlow, a Clarissa to a Lovelace, or Ahab to his own white whale does not bind the characters to Singer in *The Heart Is a Lonely Hunter*.

On a realistic level there are other small problems as well. Several of the episodes in the middle section of the novel are either irrelevant or gratuitous to the main lines of the action (I am thinking of the shooting of Baby Wilson, Blount's encounter with the crazed evangelist, the riot at the amusement park; but others could be mentioned). Occasionally, characters are given dialogue so preposterous that it would bring high color to the face of a Victorian melodramatist: Copeland, who reads Spinoza and Shakespeare, says "Pshaw and double pshaw" when goaded into anger. Several times in the novel people express frustration and rage by hitting their heads against walls, fists against tables, thighs against stones. And, finally, climactic scenes collapse because the writer is too busy establishing lofty poetic meaning to notice the absurdity of a literal image. Here, for instance, is Biff's final recognition on the last page of the book: "Between the two worlds he was suspended. He saw that he was looking at his own face in the counter glass before him. Sweat glistened on his temples and his face was contorted. One eye was opened wider than the other. The left eye delved narrowly into the past while the right gazed wide and affrighted into a future of blackness, error, and ruin. And he was suspended between radiance and darkness. Between bitter irony and faith." Like the legendary student who wrote of Petrarch standing with one foot in the Renaissance while with the other he spanned the Middle Ages, Mrs. McCullers has forgotten the classic rule: specify first; signify later.

When one remembers, however, that *The Heart Is a Lonely Hunter* is the work of a twenty-two-year-old girl, the realistic lapses are understandable; they could easily be corrected by more careful observation and growth. But the failures on the level of fable are more troublesome because they point to an ambivalence that was a permanent feature of Mrs. McCullers's sensibility. There existed in her nature a continuing conflict between her nearer and her further vision, between her desire to document the world and a desire to give it evocative poetic significance. Like Edward Albee (who—in Philip Roth's fine phrase—was "born Maupassant but wished to be Plato") she seemed to waver in her own evaluation of her gifts, and sometimes would express contradictory allegiances almost in the same breath. The most remarkable and revealing example of this occurs in a set of notes on writing, "The Flowering Dream," published in *Esquire* in 1959. First, she tells an anecdote that confirms her existence on a plane beyond mundane reality: "What to know and what not to know? John Brown, from the American Embassy, was here to visit, and he pointed his long forefinger and said, 'I admire you, Carson, for your ignorance.' I said, 'Why?' He asked, 'When was the Battle of Hastings, and what was it about? . . . I said, 'John, I don't think I care much.' He said, 'That's what I mean. You don't clutter your mind with the facts of life.' " But then, two paragraphs later, comes this expression of the ultimate supremacy of living facts in fiction: "Every day, I read the *New York Daily News*, and very soberly. It is interesting to know the name of the lover's lane where the stabbing took place, and the circumstances which the *New York Times* never reports. In that unsolved murder in Staten Island, it is interesting to know that the doctor and his wife, when they were stabbed, were wearing Mormon nightgowns, three-quarter length. Lizzie Borden's breakfast, on the sweltering summer day she killed her father, was mutton soup. Always details provoke more ideas than any generality could furnish. When Christ was pierced in His *left side*, it is more moving and evocative than if He were just pierced."

The trouble with the symbolism of *The Heart Is a Lonely Hunter* begins with Mrs. McCullers's inability to decide whether Singer is pierced on his left side, just pierced, or never pierced at all. The characters themselves are rarely in doubt. For Mick Kelly, the thought of God conjures up an image of Mr. Singer with a long white sheet around him, and she whispers: "Lord forgiveth me, for I knoweth not what I do." Preparing her lesson for the Sunday school, Alice Brannon chooses the text "All men seek for Thee"; and a moment later, reflecting on the gathering of the disciples, her husband thinks of the mute. Gradually, however, the correspondences become rather murky. Copeland's daughter, Portia, claims that Singer's shirts are as white as if John the Baptist wore them; and as the plot thickens, the mute becomes poignantly and comically all things to all men: a Jew to the Hebrews, a Turk to the Turks, a wizard to the ignorant. Obviously, Mrs. McCullers wants us to see Singer as an ironic God figure, a product of mass wish-fulfillment; but even an ironic symbol runs the danger of becoming too indiscriminately resonant. Part of the problem stems from Mrs. McCullers's flawed control over the implications of the symbol itself. Usually, the insistence on Singer's religious nature is made by one of his blinded admirers, but sometimes the objective narrator seems to confirm their romantic obsessions. Singer, Mrs. McCullers writes, has "the look of peace that is seen most often in those who are very wise or very sorrowful." And finally, the mute is thirty-three when he dies, a detail chosen not by Blount or Mick Kelly, but by the author.

Some of the same uneasiness must greet the frequent assertion that *The Heart Is a Lonely Hunter* is an allegory about fascism. Although Mrs. McCullers has given this reading her guarded blessing, its origin is difficult to pinpoint. I suspect, however, that it may have grown from the casual remark of Clifton Fadiman, who—in his early notice—confessed to seeing signs of a myth of fascist and anti-fascist forces in the human soul. Yet, even if we recall Mrs. McCullers's cautious disclaimer ("the word is used here in its very broadest terms . . . the spiritual rather than the political side of that phenomenon") the analogy has no roots in the narrative. In what sense does Singer actively tyrannize anyone; who is being regimented, and to what degree? Can Christ and Hitler live comfortably within the confines of the same myth?

What we have here, I think, is early evidence of Mrs. McCullers's susceptibility to portent, her tendency to glide irresistibly toward any beckoning abstraction so long as it is somber, suggestive, and poetic. She never wrote a book that was not to some degree weakened by this inclination, and only once (in *The Ballad of the Sad Café*) was she able to put dark fancy to the service of a compelling and powerful literal truth. In *The Member of the Wedding*, her finest achievement, there is less aberrant symbolizing than in any of her other works.

Yet even after all the damaging charges have been made, *The Heart Is a Lonely Hunter* remains what it was in 1940: "a queer sad book that sticks in the mind." The original design is brilliant enough not to be wholly dimmed by the failure of the performance. If the inflated myth finally collapses, the sense of small-town meanness holds up. Few books of the 1930s communicate as well the stagnancy of life in a depressed textile community and the inevitable frustration for those who try to stir free from it. "Find an octopus and put socks on it," says Blount in a phrase that sums up a generation. If the solemnity of the novel palls, the flashes of shrewd country humor remain bright: the antics of Grandpa Copeland and his ancient mule Lee Jackson; the fancies of Bubber Kelly, who prefers fairy tales that have something to eat in them. If Brannon and Copeland seem flat, Mick Kelly is about as round as a twelve-year-old can be. Laughter has always been the finest defense against pretentiousness, and in her treatment of several minor characters and of Mick herself, Mrs. McCullers reveals an affectionate gaiety that provides wholesome leavening for the pessimism so pervasive in this first novel.

The portrait of Mick Kelly is a charming evocation of the sensitivity and thickness, the exuberance and boredom, the ease of flight and quickness of descent that mark a familiar period in early adolescence. Like so many characters in Mrs. McCullers's books, Mick is defined by the extremity of her isolation and the fever of her fantasy life. Although she wants desperately to connect with other people, she cultivates those qualities of talent and personality that might bring her increased separateness as well as applause. Excitement keeps her imagination at boiling point. To escape the squalor of her slum environment, she climbs a ladder to the roof of a house being built nearby and sits reflecting on the possibilities of celebrity and fortune. In her inventor's phase, she hopes to market radios the size of green peas that people could stick in their ears and to provide flying machines to fit comfortably on a voyager's back. During her heroic period, she expresses her desires in murals of natural and human catastrophe, "Town Burning," or "Sea Gull with Back Broken in Storm." In her interlude as a composer, she hopes to rival Mozart in symphony and song, but since her family cannot afford an instrument, she tries to make a violin out of a broken ukulele. Her tunes, dissonant and intense, carry titles like "Africa," "The Snowstorm," "A Big Fight." The magnilloquent but unfinished "This Thing I Want, I Know Not What" is her masterpiece.

As the conflict worsens between the world and her imagination, Mick constructs her most elaborate and personal defense: "She sat down on the steps and laid her head on her knees. She went into the inside room. With her it was like there was two places—the inside room and the outside room. School and the family and the things that happened every day were in the outside room. Mister Singer was in both rooms. Foreign countries and plans and music were in the inside room. The songs she thought about were there. And the symphony." A moment later, Mrs. McCullers conveys the transparent frailty of her defense with the sentence: "Spareribs stuck his dirty hand up to her eyes because she had been staring off at space. She slapped him."

Although Mick is irrepressibly creative, she is by no means free from an egotism strident enough to injure others. When her brother accidently shoots Baby Wilson, she torments him with visions of Sing Sing and hellfire; and we are told earlier that she had continually hit him whenever she noticed his hands in his pants, so that now he never "peed normal like other kids" but with his hands behind him. Although Mick is a virtuoso of escape, her artistry is rarely effective, and at the end of the novel she feels the disquiet of being barred from the inside room. She does, however, manage to express a qualified affirmation, which—in its vernacular familiarity—is one of the most convincing moments of celebration in the novel:

> But maybe it would be true about the piano and turn out O.K.
> Maybe she would get a chance soon. Else what the hell good had
> it all been—the way she felt about music and the plans she had
> made in the inside room? It had to be some good if anything made
> sense. . . .
>   All right!
>   O.K.!
>   Some good.

Part of Mick's appeal rests in her indomitability and it is this sense of a human being refusing to accept meanness that Mrs. McCullers is able to celebrate so skillfully. Singer talking blissfully with his hands to an incomprehending Antonapoulos; the feuding Kelly family joined for a short while in loyalty and love; the weary Copeland hearing "rich, dark sounds" from the pages of Spinoza —these are moments of beauty as well as pathos. Rage, anger, and indignation are often in this story the other side of love, for Mrs. McCullers—like Keats—believed that a street fight is ugly, but the energies displayed can be beautiful.

No such beauty exists in *Reflections in a Golden Eye*, the most pompous and disagreeable of all her books. Almost as if to spite those critics who complained of the squalor of her subject matter, Mrs. McCullers created a swamp where no light shines and no people live. In 1941, when the novel first appeared, reviewers intensified their earlier objections to the morbidity of her materials: perversion, voyeurism, mutilation, and murder; but now, three decades and many a Gothic novel later, the objection is not to the luridness of the subject, but rather to lack of artistry in Mrs. McCullers's treatment. *Reflections in a Golden Eye* is a muddled, pretentious book that promises to illuminate shadowy places of the human psyche, but manages only to exploit them.

The scene is an army camp in the deep South during the late 1930s, and the characters (to quote the best line in the book) are "two officers, a soldier, two women, a Filipino, and a horse." One officer is Captain Penderton, a tightly repressed latent homosexual, infatuated with his wife's lovers; the other is Major Langdon, an easygoing charmboy who bedded the lusty Leonora Penderton in a blackberry patch two hours after their first meeting. The soldier, a moronic naif named Williams, sees Mrs. Penderton framed nude in a window and begins tiptoeing into her bedroom to worship her while she sleeps. The other woman, Alison Langdon, frail and neurasthenic, has recently clipped off her nipples with a garden shears, and now finds solace in the company of a prancing houseboy, Anacleto. The horse, Firebird, is tended by Williams, adored by Leonora, and despised by her husband. After a series of violent, inconclusive adventures, Penderton is drawn in love and hate toward the silent Williams; but when he finds that the private has eyes only for his wife, he murders him.

After such action, what explanation but fantasy? And recently a number of critics have argued that *Reflections in a Golden Eye* is not supposed to be read literally, but rather as a deliberately extravagant symbolic prose poem, true not to the real world but to the vagaries of abnormal psychology. In its charity, however, this argument ignores the fact that the novel never establishes credible connections with any world, literal or fantastic, and that its understanding of human pathology is misty to the point of meaninglessness. As often happens in Mrs. McCullers's weakest books, the fatal devils are an overriding ambition and something less than full clarity of intention. Her basic subject is clear enough: the ravages of dammed-up sexual energies; but in a desire to marry Faulkner to Flaubert and D. H. Lawrence, she takes three mutually contradictory attitudes toward her subject matter. First, as an objective narrator, she introduces the action in a detached and formal manner: short sentences, sculptured paragraphs, a poised monotonic response to everything miraculous and mundane. Designed to establish the verisimilitude of the story, this style depends on a great many details drawn from a firsthand experience of army life—matters of rank, architecture, armor, and so on. Existing simultaneously with the reporter is a satirist, whose aim is to demolish everyone in sight for the assorted vices of pride, moral vacancy, and self-deceit. Leonora is shown to be so dim-witted that the demands of writing a thank-you note reduce her to nervous exhaustion; her husband, a storehouse of technical information, cannot put two facts together to make an idea, and is entirely blind to the most obvious of his own physiological impulses; the mindless Major Langdon orders his life on the premise that only two things matter: "to be a good animal and to serve my country"; and young Williams, when driven to the point of action, finds "the vaporish impressions within him condensed to a thought." The third voice in the novel belongs to a mythopoeic explorer who sees in this grotesque domestic drama a monumental conflict of will against instinct, the artificial against the natural, and death against life.

The journalist and the satirist do their work only too well. By concentrating on the facts of the physical and social scene, Mrs. McCullers makes it impossible for us not to ask that her human beings remain plausible; but by insisting that the people are pathological types, and by damning them with such relentless sarcasm, she makes it difficult for us to care for their inhumanities. There is excessive malice, too, in the mockery. Usually, satire achieves force by aiming at targets that represent some universal yet remedial failing (the self-interest of politicians, the heartlessness of society women, the greed of bankers); but Mrs. Mc-Cullers's satire deals with perverse emotional failures of which the characters themselves are unaware, or about which they can do nothing (Penderton's unconscious desire for a handsome young primitive; Williams's witlessness, and so on).

It is, however, only when the poet takes over that Mrs. McCullers reveals the full inadequacy of her conception, since she has neither the language nor the depth of insight to give the sordid drama the elemental force of myth. Different as they are, the voices of the realist, the satirist, and the mythmaker can exist compatibly in a single work (*St. Mawr* and *Heart of Darkness* are modern examples) but in Lawrence and Conrad the ordinary people are free agents and the narrator's analysis of their situation is weighty enough to give them a significance beyond the realm of the natural. In Mrs. McCullers's book, the people are caricatures and the narrator's commentary is a triumph of adjectives over analysis, reminiscent of the worst in Poe rather than the best in Lawrence. Penderton and Williams continually move in states between stupor and somnambulism, experiencing rootless terror and dark, unspeakable desires. When the captain is near the private, he suffers "a curious lapse of sensory impressions" and finds himself "unable to see or hear properly"; and Williams often stands silent staring ominously into space "in the attitude of one who listens to a call from a long distance." Unfortunately, the call never comes through for Williams, or for the reader; the menace remains obscure and Mrs. McCullers's promptings stir only laughter and disbelief.

In the last analysis, *Reflections in a Golden Eye* provides no genuine insight into sexual pathologies, but merely an arbitrary series of gaudy, melodramatic episodes that shock without illuminating and never coalesce into larger patterns of action or meaning. Penderton may drop a kitten into a freezing mailbox, but his sadism seems less significant than his stupidity. Williams, standing over the sleeping body of Leonora, finishes her half-eaten piece of chicken; we may remember the gesture, but not the true nature of the man who made it. When Alison sees the soldier hiding in the shadows of the Penderton house, she feels "an eerie shock," closes her eyes, and counts "by sevens to two hundred and eighty." People counting by seven to two hundred and eighty—this is a useful image to describe what goes on in *Reflections in a Golden Eye*—strange, oddly provocative, but not very enlightening about human character and conduct.

The Ballad of the Sad Café is a good deal more rewarding. Instead of trying to compete with writers of much greater psychological awareness and architechtonic skill, Mrs. McCullers here wisely moves in a limited area more suited to her talents—the alien, elemental world of legend and romance. Like all good ballads, her story is urgent, atmospheric, and primitive, and yet, in its melodramatic swiftness and simplicity, tells us more things memorable about human life than all the devious sophisticated posturings of *Reflections in a Golden Eye*.

In the background are the physical facts of life that count for so much in the ballad world: a dingy southern town cut off from the accommodations of civilized society, boundaries of swamps and cold black pinewood, weather that is raw in winter and white with the glare of heat in summer. Only those who must come here: the tax collector to bother the rich; an investigator to refuse credit to Ryan, the weaver; a lost traveler to find his way back to his destination. Decayed buildings lean in imminent collapse and intimations of mortality are everywhere. The moon makes "dim, twisted shadows on the blossoming peach trees," and the odor of sweet spring grass mingles with the warm, sour smell of a nearby lagoon. Strangers arrive suddenly, often at night, and they have intimate ties with the twilight world of animals. The hunchback's hands are like "dirty sparrow claws," and he perches on a railing the way "a sick bird huddles on a telephone wire," to "grieve publicly." Much depends on the cycle of the seasons and the climactic events of the plot often have their effective climatic correspondences. Autumn begins with cool days of a "clean bright sweetness," but when the villain comes home from prison, the weather turns sticky, sultry, and rotten. A month before the famous wrestling match that brings the story to a close, snow falls for the first time in living memory.

The boldness and precision with which she creates the sense of a town estranged from the rest of the world is the first of Mrs. McCullers's successes in *The Ballad of the Sad Café*. Unlike those narrators in the earlier novels who move uneasily from realism to myth and back again, the invented voice in this story has an obvious authority and grace. Beginning simply in the present, she tells us that things are dismal now but once upon a time there was gaiety and color in the human landscape. No attempt is made to mask the calamitous outcome; ruin is announced at the start; our interest will be entirely in how it was accomplished. Since she is confident in her grasp of the moment and the milieu, Mrs. McCullers assumes a relaxed, colloquial style, punctuating the narrative with phrases like "time must pass" and "so do not forget."

Knowing that her gruesome story might, if too solemnly told, seem wildly melodramatic, she skillfully uses folk humor to sweeten the Gothic tale. When the shambling, toothless Merlie Ryan spreads the rumor that Amelia has murdered the newly arrived Lymon, Mrs. McCullers casually reports: "It was a fierce and sickly tale the town built up that day. In it were all the things which cause the heart to shiver—a hunchback, a midnight burial in the swamp, the dragging of Miss Amelia through the streets of the town." But then, moments later, she parades her little peacock proudly down the stairs. Throughout the narrative, understatement and playfulness humanize the actors and make their behavior seem less morbid. Often, in dialogue, they use an idiom full of the comic hyperbole so common in country speech. Amelia claims to have slept as soundly as if she were drowned in axle grease, and when she is dizzy with apprehension and love, the neighbors speak of her being "well on her way . . . up fools' hill," and they can't wait to see how the affair will turn out.

It turns out badly. *The Ballad of the Sad Café* is the story of Miss Amelia Evans, a quirky amazon who sells feed, guano, and domestic staples in the town's only thriving store. Tall, dark, and unapproachable in a rough, masculine way, Amelia is an uncompromising merchant with a passion for vindictive lawsuits and a beneficent witch doctor with a genuine desire to ease human pain. Both her business acumen and her healing powers are legendary; what she shrewdly extracts in trade she gives back in the free and effective dispensation of a hundred different cures. Since her liquors relieve melancholy, her foods hunger, and her folk remedies pain, this perverse cross between Ceres, Bacchus, and the neighborhood medicine man is the one indispensable person in town.

That the hard-fisted Amelia has the living touch is demonstrated at the arrival of a sniveling hunchbacked dwarf who asks for food and shelter. His worth, he claims, is based on the urgency of kinship, and his weird unraveling of cousins, half sisters, and third husbands is a neat parody of the mysterious genealogical links in ballad and romance. Miss Amelia immediately acknowledges the tie, lightly touches his hump, and offers him liquor, dinner, and a bed. Soon, Cousin Lymon is installed in Amelia's sanctuary, sharing rooms rarely seen by living eyes, and a bizarre relationship, very much like love, transforms them both. As lover, she becomes softened, graceful, communicative, eager to extend the rewards of companionship to others; he, the beloved, becomes proud, perky, aristocratic. Even the townspeople benefit. The liquor that Miss Amelia used to dispense on her doorstep is now served inside, and gradually the store evolves into a café featuring the exotic hunchback and some palatable food and drink. Warmth, affectionate fellowship, "a certain gaiety and grace of behavior," momentarily replace suspicion, loneliness, egotism, and rough-hewn malice—the rigorous truths of the world outside. Niggardly Amelia puts free crackers on the counter, customers share their liquor, and the flourishing café provides the one bright page in the history of this melancholy town.

Unhappily, the festive interlude lasts only six years before the sins of the past exact their tribute and the catastrophe announced at the start is set in motion. Some years before the appearance of Lymon, the young Amelia had been married for ten stormy days to Marvin Macy. Handsome, mercurial, vicious, and cunning, Macy had been a most notable young scoundrel, the demon lover of every "soft-eyed" young girl in town. Miraculously enough, *he* had fallen passionately in love with the haggard Amelia and became her long-suffering romantic knight. As a disdainful mistress, Amelia needed little instruction; after their marriage, she rejected his advances, sold his presents, and battered his face with her punches. Macy, disconsolate and swearing vengeance, ran off to a life of crime and an eventual stretch in the Atlanta penitentiary. Afterwards, Miss Amelia cut up his Klansman's robe to cover her tobacco plants.

Once Macy reappears in town, the tempo quickens and everyone prepares for the inevitable confrontation of the two epic antagonists. Most of the wise money is on Amelia, for she had beaten more than her weight several times before. The twist, however, in this tale is provided by Cousin Lymon, who completes the eccentric triangle of love relationships by falling desperately for the roguish Macy. This time it is Amelia's turn to suffer at the hands of a capricious beloved. While Lymon slavishly follows the scornful Macy about town, she becomes increasingly distraught at the turn in his affections; but nothing can be done. Lymon announces that Macy will move in with them and Amelia comes to the mournful recognition that "once you have lived with another . . . it is better to take in your mortal enemy than face the terror of living alone."

Step by step, Amelia and Macy prepare for the hand-to-hand combat that everyone knows must come. On the second of February, when a bloody-breasted hawk gives the signal by flying over Amelia's house, all the townspeople move as spectators toward the café. At seven o'clock, the two contestants begin to pound one another with hundreds of bone-cracking blows. After a savage half-hour, when boxing has turned to wrestling, Amelia puts her triumphant hands to the throat of her fallen adversary; but with astonishing swiftness, Cousin Lymon flies at her back, pulls her off, and gives the victory to Macy. That night, to celebrate their triumph, the two men smash up Amelia's property and disappear. In the months that follow, Amelia lets the café and her healing practice fall into ruin, and she eventually becomes a recluse. The town returns to its desolate, mechanical ways; "the soul rots with boredom", and the tale ends with the swelling song of a chain gang.

Much of what is permanently haunting in this grotesque little story is the product of Mrs. McCullers's easy relationship with the properties of the ballad world. Experience heightened far beyond the realm of plausibility is given a valid, poetic truth by the propriety of those conventions that make the miraculous seem oddly real. Dreams, superstitions, omens, numbers, musical motifs, all operate here to provide an authentic atmosphere for this perverse triangle of passions, and to make the inexplicable longings of the characters seem like dark elemental forces in the natural world. Enigmatic melodies are heard in the night: wild, high voices singing songs that never end. Macy, the demon lover, plays the guitar, and when he sings the tunes glide "slowly from his throat like eels." As a doctor, Amelia depends on a stunning variety of secret herbs; her Kroup Kure, made from whiskey, rock candy, and an unnamed third power, is a wonder drug, while her liquor has been known to bring up messages from the bottom of the human soul. When she guards the low fire of her ritual still, Amelia likes to untie knots in rope, and in her parlor cabinet she keeps an acorn and two small stones. The acorn she picked from the ground the day her father died, and the stones had once been removed from her kidney. If she wants Lymon to come along to Chee-haw, she asks him seven times and when he continually refuses, she draws a heavy line with a stick around the barbecue pit and orders him not to trespass that limit. Naturally, when the time must be set for the epic fight, seven o'clock is chosen. Miss Amelia is not the only character to be given a powerful armory of signs and talismans. Lymon sits regularly on a sack of guano and is rarely without his snuffbox. Years earlier, Macy had courted his love with a bunch of swamp flowers, a sack of chitterlings, and a silver ring; and when he returns from prison the neighbors fear him as more dangerous than ever because while put away he "must have learned the method of laying charms." Always called devilish, Macy never sweats, not even in August, and that—Mrs. McCullers reminds us—is surely "a sign worth pondering."

By relying so heavily on charms and rituals, the characters emphasize the fated, irrational quality of so many of their decisive acts. Like most works in its traditional genre, *The Ballad of the Sad Café* illustrates the consequences of moral choice but does not probe it; analysis is less vital than the starkness of dramatic presentation. Yet an evocative atmosphere and a strong story line would not in themselves ensure success if the illustration were not thematically absorbing as well. The richly patterned, sinister dance in which Macy, Amelia, and Lymon play at different times the roles of lover and beloved dramatizes the wayward nature of human passion and the irreconcilable antagonism inherent in every love relationship.

At one point in his poem "Prayer for My Daughter," William Butler Yeats, speaking of the splendid contrariety with which females choose their lovers, describes how beautiful women sometimes eat "a crazy salad with their meat." *The Ballad of the Sad Café* is about the "crazy salad" of every man: ugly and beautiful, heiress and outlaw, dwarf and amazon—they all choose love objects in ways that demonstrate that passion is the most permanent and amazing of all the human mysteries. In the McCullers world, the lover occupies the highest seat in the pantheon, for he has the restlessness and imagination to wish to break free from the constrictive prison of ego and connect with another person. His choices are often arbitrary and improbable, but once made he worships them with a constancy that can only inspire amazement. Everyone wants to be a lover because the lover is the archetypal creative spirit: dreamer, quester, romantic idealist. If love compels, it can also soften. When Macy is smitten with Amelia, he becomes improved in civility; and Amelia's passion for Lymon not only refines her temperament and reduces her lawsuits, but results in the establishment of the café. Product of her love, the café is the symbol of the ability of human affection to create intimacy and delight where only barrenness existed before. Yet, if love can sweeten and refine, it can also leave the lover defenseless. Having created the beloved in the image of his own desperate desire, the lover is open to rebuff and betrayal, for he tempts the one permanent quality of any beloved—his cruelty. In *The Ballad of the Sad Café*, the beloved is a static figure, chosen by someone else. Easily resentful of being considered a token, he is also quick to recognize the assailability of his admirer and the extent of his own manipulative powers.

In Mrs. McCullers's triangle, each character is revealed successively in the roles of lover and beloved. In his suit of Amelia, Macy is meek with longing and easily swayed by others: he saves his wages, abandons fornication, and goes regularly to church. But in response to Amelia's chilling rejection, he becomes more brutally antisocial than he had ever been before. On his return to town, cast as his wife's revenger and Lymon's beloved, he alternates between abusiveness and complete indifference, calling the sullen dwarf "Brokeback" at one moment and ignoring him the next. Like Macy, Lymon is also violently contradictory in both roles. Admired by Amelia, he gains forceful self-assurance, but also learns to exercise the hateful tyranny of a spoiled child. Finicky, boastful, self-absorbed, he becomes wildly obsessive in his demands for personal gratification. Yet when he falls for Macy, his reversal is perhaps even more disagreeable. Obsessed now by his desire to attract Macy's attention, he flaps his ears and mopes about pathetically like a small dog sick for love.

The most memorable metamorphosis, however, is experienced by Amelia. Chosen by Macy at nineteen, she spits in contempt and strikes out fiercely at every opportunity. Hardhearted, peremptory, and self-sufficient, she does not let her rage affect her capacity to turn a deal in her own favor, and she quickly strips her husband of everything he owns. At thirty, however, when she chooses Lymon, a remarkable change occurs. The rudest misanthrope in town turns genial, even cheerful, moving easily among people, sharing her liquor, forgetting to bolt the door at night. Instead of overalls and swampboots, she occasionally dons a soft red dress, and as she rubs Lymon twice a day with pot liquor to give him strength, her hatred of physicality relaxes. Suddenly nostalgic about the past, she turns candid about the present, confiding in the dwarf about trade secrets and the size of her bank account. As lover for the first time in her life, Amelia takes emotional risks by putting herself in a position of extreme vulnerability. Staring at Lymon, her face wears the fascinating expression of "pain, perplexity, and uncertain joy"—the lonesome look of the lover. When she learns that Macy may return, she—in her pride—miscalculates Lymon's fickleness and her own power over his life; and after his affection is alienated, she becomes frightfully distracted, pursuing those contradictory courses that lead to her downfall.

Because she has the capacity to change and the energy to pursue her awakened desire for companionship, Amelia turns from a harridan evoking awe to a woman worthy of compassion. By learning to love she has become more human—more tender, gracious, amiable, perceptive; but also more obviously exposed to the inevitable stings of loneliness, betrayal, and suffering. As healer, hostess, and lover, she is—despite her rudeness and suspicion—a force for good in the community, and the destruction of her dream is a cause for genuine mourning. *The Ballad of the Sad Café* is an elegy for Amelia Evans, and it has all the brooding eloquence and eccentricity to stand as a fitting tribute to that very peculiar lady.

RICHARD M. COOK

Reflections in a Golden Eye

In her novel *Reflections in a Golden Eye*, published in 1941, McCullers describes a world where the suffering imposed by isolation is unrelieved by the possibility of human idealism and individual struggle. It is a stark, blank world devoid of love and charm, where life exists on its lowest instinctual level. Tennessee Williams has written that "*Reflections in a Golden Eye* is one of the purest and most powerful of those works which are conceived in that Sense of The Awful which is the desperate black root of nearly all significant modern art, from the Guernica of Picasso to the cartoons of Charles Addams." To evoke this "Sense of the Awful" McCullers has substituted the impersonality of an army post for the varieties of a southern Main Street. She has restrained her gift for the humorous and pathetic detail in the interests of a more austere tone and a tighter more rapidly moving plot. And she has transformed human oddity from a mark of the individual personality into a sign of general human perversion. *Reflections in a Golden Eye* is a short, violent drama about people so mired in their deviancy, so trapped by what Ihab Hassan has called "instinctual necessity," and so bereft of all humor and hope, as to be beyond redemption as valuable, living personalities. Caught up in their dreary routine and driven by compulsions they do not understand, they appear to us more as shadows than people grotesque reflections, who may evoke in some readers a sense of the awful but lack the substance to involve us in their suffering or make us seriously care for their fate.

The story takes place on a southern army post during peacetime. It is a dull place where any unusual event is certain to attract attention; and it is as repressive as it is dull. A spirit of mindless conformity pervades the post tending to

From *Carson McCullers*. © 1975 by Frederick Ungar Publishing Co., Inc.

regulate all behavior and thought according to the drab official standards of military protocol. The physical layout of the post reflects its mechanical, inhuman spirit: "The huge, concrete barracks, the neat rows of officers' homes, built one precisely like the other, the gym, the chapel, the golf course, and the swimming pools—all is designed according to a certain rigid pattern." In such an environment, an environment where every man "is expected only to follow the heels ahead of him," all human expression takes on the stamp of a general impersonality, while sexual relations turn particularly remote and impersonal, resembling more the blind reactions of brute instinct than expressions of individual human love. The blank repressive sameness of army life establishes a standard of behavior in the novel that no "normal" person can conform to. On this particular army post the adjusted appear as deviant as the maladjusted.

Leonora Penderton and her lover Major Langdon are the two characters most happily adapted to life on the post. Leonora, who lacks the intelligence to write a thank-you note and "could not have multiplied twelve by thirteen under threat of the rack," spends her time riding her stallion Firebird, dreaming of turkey dinners, and making love to the major. The voluptuous wife of the impotent Captain Penderton, she is known as a great lady on the post. Her stupidity either goes unnoticed or is considered an asset. She calls the general "Old Sugar" to his face, "and the General, like most of the officers on the post, fairly ate out of her hand." Leonora is the only thoroughly good-natured character in the novel. Yet her lack of spite and guile obviously derives more from a deficiency of the head than a largeness of heart. She lacks the wit to be mean.

Major Langdon may be more intelligent than his mistress, but he rarely shows it. Langdon, who first made love to Leonora in a blackberry patch two hours after they met, is a reckless, insensitive philistine and brute. Whereas Leonora is merely mindless, Langdon is a threat to mind and to all expressions of a civilized taste. He scorns his wife's interest in classical music: "To me it's like swallowing a bunch of angle-worms," and bullies her artistic, effete houseboy, Anacleto, with the threat of military service: "God! You're a rare bird! What I wouldn't do if I could get you in my battalion!" Riding horses, bedding Leonora, and following orders, constitute a life style that is not mere habit to Langdon but a personal directive and a primitive norm that embodies all the values in his world: "Only two things matter to me now—to be a good animal and to serve my country. A healthy body and patriotism."

If military life has been a blessing to Langdon, it has been a curse to his wife. Sensitive, artistic, and eccentric, Alison Langdon has been so badly scarred by her husband's neglect and cruelty and the army's repressive brutality that she has come to despise herself and her sex. Deranged by grief over the death of her deformed child (her husband would not touch it because it was deformed), Alison, shortly before the novel opens, has cut off her nipples with the garden shears. It was an act repudiating her sex and her life. She lies in bed throughout most of the novel and finally dies in an asylum to which she has been sent by her husband.

Despite her suffering, it is difficult to take Alison very seriously. She has survived so long as an utterly hopeless wreck that there seems to be nothing left to save. Yet she is important in the novel as she is the only person to possess sufficient intelligence and detachment to look at the events and the people on the post critically. Her suffering has sharpened not dulled her sensibilities, and she judges what she sees, including her own condition, with a vindictive accuracy born of her pain:

> Everyone she had known in the past five years was somehow wrong.
> . . . Morris Langdon [her husband] in his blunt way was as stupid and heartless as a man could be. Leonora was nothing but an animal. And thieving Weldon Penderton was at bottom hopelessly corrupt. What a Gang! Even she herself she loathed. If it were not for sordid procrastination and if she had a rag of pride, she and Anacleto would not be in this house tonight.

Alison is important to the novel as a living example of the outrageous victimization inflicted on the human spirit by intolerance and brutishness. But she is also important as a counterconsciousness, a sensibility in impotent rebellion against the stupid animality of her husband and the empty repressive ritual of military life.

The most interesting and complicated character in the book is Captain Weldon Penderton. He is also one of the most extreme cases of eclectic deviancy to appear in modern American literature. Besides being impotent and homosexual, Penderton is a sado masochist, a fetishist, and an incipient drug addict. His more petty deviancies include stealing silver spoons and hiding them in his truss box, stuffing little kittens into freezing mailboxes, and circulating vicious rumors about his closest acquaintances. Yet for all the sensational excessiveness of McCullers's portrait, she has created in Penderton a character with a problem too serious and too central in her vision of human nature to be easily dismissed as a mere freak. Penderton is quite possibly the most thoroughly isolated character that McCullers ever created. So removed is he from the lives of those around him, and so out of touch with any honestly felt human emotion, that he might pass as an exaggerated contrivance, an experiment in sheer grotesque characterization, were it not for the fact that deep within his troubled consciousness Penderton senses his alienation and at moments has the courage to see it for what it is.

As with everyone else in the novel, Penderton's personality owes much of its distinctness to the shaping influences of the military setting. The army has been a place of retreat for him. He escaped into it as a means of establishing an identity

—an identity that his ambivalent sexual attitudes have denied him: "Sexually, the captain obtained within himself a delicate balance between the male and female elements, with the susceptibility of both sexes and the active powers of neither." Without the inclination or the capacity to pursue an active masculine role in the world Penderton has assumed a semiascetic existence as an army career officer. His rank and uniform ("The Captain always wore uniform when away from the post") have provided him with a mask of impersonality and an official government-approved identity. Yet it is an identity that the captain can only partially accept. For dependent as he is on his military image, Penderton has moments when he sees how fraudulent that identity is and how restrictive and inhuman its dimensions. In a conversation with Major Langdon about Anacleto's antic behavior he finds himself suddenly rebelling against the major's complacent clichés on the advantages of conforming:

> "You mean," Captain Penderton said, "that any fulfillment obtained at the expense of normalcy is wrong, and should not be allowed to bring happiness. In short, it is better, because it is morally honorable, for the square peg to keep scraping about the round hole rather than to discover and use the unorthodox square that would fit it?"
>
> "Why, you put it exactly right," the Major said. "Don't you agree with me?"
>
> "No," said the Captain, after a short pause. With gruesome vividness the Captain suddenly looked into his soul and saw himself. For once he did not see himself as others saw him; there came to him a distorted doll-like image, mean of countenance and grotesque in form. The Captain dwelt on this vision without compassion. He accepted it with neither alteration nor excuse. "I don't agree," he repeated absently.

But if Penderton recognises his doll-like insubstantiality, he can do very little to change himself. At two points in the novel he tries to break out of his toy-soldier image, to somehow make contact with a more vital, authentic nature than his own that might save him from his false, dead self. Both attempts are disastrous. Trapped in his thwarted sexuality, driven by urges that revolt him, Captain Penderton strives for a physical involvement he can never enjoy. In the end he succeeds only in hurting those around him and exacerbating his already pathological state of mind.

Penderton's first attempt to break out of his shell occurs when he tries to ride Firebird. Seeing in the horse a spirited animality he despairs of, Penderton, though a terrible horseman, feels compelled to confront Firebird's raw strength, to test himself against its brute animal nature. Without realizing what he is doing, he goads Firebird into a blind gallop that he finds both terrifying and momentarily liberating. As the horse plunges madly along a narrow path through the woods,

> three words were in the Captain's heart. He shaped them soundlessly with trembling lips, as if he had not breath to spare a whisper: "I am lost."

And having given up life, the Captain suddenly began to live. A great mad joy surged through him. This emotion, coming as unexpectedly as the plunge of the horse when he had broken away, was one that the Captain had never experienced. . . . He was conscious of the pure keen air and he felt the marvel of his own tense body, his laboring heart, and the miracle of blood, muscle, nerves and bone. The Captain knew no terror now.

But Penderton's delirious joy, which seems to come from a sudden feeling of oblivious physical involvement, quickly changes into vicious hatred. Upon finally bringing Firebird to a halt, he beats him bloody with a stick and then drops to the ground in a fit of weeping. The wild ride on Firebird leaves him empty, broken, and more isolated than ever: "Out in the forest there, the Captain looked like a broken doll that had been thrown away." Done without intention or plan the whole act had been essentially meaningless—a spasmodic jerk that struck out wildly only to recoil on itself in pain and exhaustion. Penderton's desire to make contact with a vitalizing physical energy is a need he cannot relate to the real world. It remains a compulsion, a blind alien force stripped of intentionality and control. The next time it asserts itself its victim is not a horse but a human being, Private Ellgee Williams.

Private Williams, the soldier that takes care of Firebird at the stables, is a deviate with his own problems. He believes all women carry diseases that infect men and derives an apparently unnatural pleasure from contact with animals. When he rode Firebird, "there was a sensual savage smile on his lips that would have surprised his barrack mates." He is also a voyeur and spends his nights squatting by Leonora's bed watching her sleep. But to Penderton, Williams is a fascinating, sensual creature whom he finds both tempting and revolting. At first he notes Williams's presence with a mixture of mild irritability and curiosity, but after the ride on Firebird, which Williams had partly witnessed, the captain begins to feel a confused and overwhelming passion for him—a passion that is neither love nor hate, but a strange, volatile combination of the two:

> He looked at the fine, skillful hands and the tender roundness of the soldier's neck. The Captain was overcome by a feeling that both repelled and fascinated him—it was as though he and the young soldier were wrestling together naked, body to body in a fight to death.

Like the urge to ride Firebird, Captain Penderton's obsession with Williams derives at least part of its intensity from his desperate need to make contact with the sensual passionate world he has cut himself off from. With his physical grace, his golden brown body, and his daily associations with other youths Williams becomes for the captain in his isolation an emblem of his own lost physicality and of a masculine world he had never known.

> He felt himself adrift, cut off from all human influence, and he car-
> ried with him the brooding image of the young soldier much as a
> witch would hug to her bosom some cunning charm. . . . He thought
> of the soldier in terms neither of love nor hate; he was conscious only
> of the irresistible yearning to break down the barrier between them.

But the captain cannot break down the barrier. He can no more communicate his feelings to Williams than Doctor Copeland could express his to his family or Singer could his to Antonapoulos. "In his heart there coursed a wild tirade of curses, words of love, supplications and abuse. But in the end he turned away silent." Williams, in turn, hardly notices the captain.

The affair ends in violence. Discovering Williams squatting by his wife's bed one night, Captain Penderton fires two bullets through Williams's chest. But, like the wild ride on Firebird, it is a meaningless gesture, an empty reflex that leaves the captain alone and more irrelevant than before: "The Captain had slumped against the wall. In his queer coarse wrapper, he resembled a broken and dissipated monk." His passion spent, he simply ceases to function. Like a mechanical doll with its mainspring broken, the Captain suddenly loses the un-natural energy generated out of his obsession.

As the compulsive behavior of Captain Penderton indicates, McCullers in *Reflections in a Golden Eye* is dealing with a radical state of alienation at once more hopeless and more terrifying than that encountered in *The Heart Is a Lonely Hunter*. The captain is not simply frustrated and defiant in the way Doctor Copeland and Jake Blount are over their failure to realize their wishes; he is deranged, his behavior extravagant and irrational, his vision of the world distorted beyond all recognizable pattern. In McCullers's words "he had lost the primitive faculty that instinctively classifies the various sensory impressions according to their relative values." Penderton, in short, is an absurd character, his isolation a condition of his very existence, his motivation without plausible relation to the world around him. And though he has moments when he seems to see into his own twisted soul, he remains a creature apart, a grotesque human being without the ideals, hopes, and visions that go so far toward humanizing the characters in *The Heart Is a Lonely Hunter*.

McCullers has created a "Sense of The Awful" in *Reflections in a Golden Eye*. The confining impersonality and barrenness of the novel's setting, the self-destructive neuroticism of its weaker characters, the empty animality of its stronger ones, the contempt for human differences and human aspiration, all depict the horrors of a modern, regimented hell—a nightmare world of isolation, repression, boredom, and violence. Communication fails in such a world, not because the characters, like those in *The Heart Is a Lonely Hunter*, have so much to say they go mad with trying to say it, but because in their resigned and unregenerate states they have lost all capacity and will to express themselves. It seems there is nothing worth saying beyond the primitive urgings of animal lust. Sex repressed or unrepressed, dominates everyone's life, its excitements and dangers holding out the only reprieve from the withering boredom of army life. Yet instead of bringing people together, sexual passion drives them further apart while the intellect and imagination rot in contempt and neglect. Like the Woolworth's store Mick finds herself in at the end of *The Heart Is a Lonely Hunter*, the army post destroys in time all hopes and plans. And the mind, devoid of any "strong, true purpose," tends toward dissolution and decay or as McCullers has written of Private Williams's mind: it is "imbued with various colors of strange tones, but without delineation, void of form."

But McCullers has sacrificed a great deal for this vision of chaos. As she wrote in the essay "The Flowering Dream," her primary method of composition was to "become the characters I write about." Much of the success of *The Heart Is a Lonely Hunter* derived from this capacity to become her characters, to leave the outside indifferent world that so easily dismisses people as niggers, objects, and freaks and enter the consciousness of the individual, bringing with her a sympathy that makes each of her characters a valuable, if extraordinary human being. In *Reflections in a Golden Eye* she has chosen to hold her characters at arm's length. She remains outside, aloof, describing their antics and compulsions with a detached, curious contempt. Thus instead of gaining that inward knowledge of loneliness and alienation that comes with a writer's sympathy or even love for her characters we are given only strange, fascinating surfaces, a mirror held up to all manner of colorful aberrations. We are in effect distracted from the pain of their sickness by the grotesquery of their symptoms. As Tennessee Williams suggested, the novel does grant a vision into the void, but a void without depth or mystery, reflecting only erratic and bizarre shapes playing on its surface.

Perhaps, indeed, the image that best characterizes this novel's vision of human nature is the one contained in its title, *Reflections in a Golden Eye*. The phrase comes from Anacleto's description of a painting he has just shown Alison Langdon. It is, he says

> "A peacock of a sort of ghastly green. With one immense golden eye.
> And in it reflections of something tiny and—" . . . "Grotesque," she
> finished for him.

Coming as it does after *The Heart Is a Lonely Hunter* with its wide-ranging, inclusive vision of man's involvement in history, politics, and love, *Reflections in a Golden Eye* presents us with a radically reduced if not, indeed, a "tiny" vision of human life. And though the book's characters may have the hard, brilliant intensity of concentrated reflections, they lack the warmth of feeling, the humor, and the psychological depth that are the result of a more complex, expansive and sympathetic view of human nature.

RICHARD GRAY

Moods and Absences

There is a peculiar quality of isolation about Carson McCullers's work, frequently remarked upon but never properly explained, that owes some of its intensity perhaps to her own status vis-à-vis the South. She does not belong to the great generation of the "renaissance," that is clear enough: indeed, she was only twelve years old when *The Sound and the Fury* was published, and her first novel, *The Heart Is a Lonely Hunter*, did not appear until after the beginning of the Second World War. But she does not really belong to the new wave of southern writers either, since apart from *Clock Without Hands*—a book dealing, among other things, with the issue of desegregation, which was not published until 1961—all of her more important fiction had been written by 1946; and was collected into a uniform edition some five years later. Her major period of creativity was very brief, consisting of about five years in all; and the last twenty or so years of her life were so marred by ill health that, in retrospect, it seems remarkable she was able to write the little, during the period, that she did. Certainly, illness offers a sufficient explanation for her gradual lapse into silence. Coming after the great fiction and poetry of the twenties and thirties, but before the more recent examples of southern Gothic (before *Wise Blood* and *Lie Down in Darkness*, for example, before even *Other Voices, Other Rooms* and *A Streetcar Named Desire*) her novels and short stories occupy, consequently, a particular transitional moment of their own in the tradition. Theirs is a special, and especially separate, place in the history of southern literature, which makes their

From *The Literature of Memory: Modern Writers of the American South.* © 1977 by Richard Gray. The Johns Hopkins University Press, 1977. Originally entitled "Southern Literature Since World War II."

author seem occasionally like one of her own characters—alone, cut off from all normal channels of communication, and strangely vulnerable.

Other factors, quite apart from her unusual literary situation, probably contributed to McCullers's interest in the dimensions of loneliness. Her childhood, for example, seems to have been a very quiet one. "Almost singularly lacking," as her biographer has put it, "in the excitement of external events," it reflected the particular milieu into which she was born; shabbily genteel, the Smith family of Columbus, Georgia, were inordinately embarrassed by their fallen circumstances and actively discouraged contact or intercourse with anybody from outside the home. Then, when Carson did grow up and move away (to New York and, later, to Europe) her aloof and rather prickly personality tended to complete the process thus begun. Always afraid of a full commitment to others, searching for the possibility of betrayal and claiming to find it even when it was not there, she seemed to draw a magic circle around herself for much of the time, and live in an inner world that was compounded equally of memory and imagination. "I . . . have my own reality," she said once toward the end of her life, made out "of language and voices and foliage"; and it was this reality, I believe, her ghostly, private world, that she tried to reproduce in most of her fiction. She gave it many names, over the years, and placed it consistently in the South. Southern though its geographical location might be, however, it was like no South anybody had ever seen before. It was not the South of newspaper articles and political speeches, nor the South of country humor or magnolia-blossom romance; it was not even the South described so extensively in the Yoknapatawpha novels. In effect, it was another country altogether, created out of all that the author had found haunting, soft, and lonely in her childhood surroundings—a new place offering a new perspective on the experience from which it had been drawn.

Perhaps we can gain a better idea of this new place, the unique map that McCullers offered of her home, by looking at one of her characteristic attempts at depicting it. Her novella, *The Ballad of the Sad Café*, for example, begins with this memorable description of a town without a name and, in doing so, establishes the climate, physical and emotional, in which all its characters are to move.

> The town itself is dreary; not much is there except the cotton-mill, the two-room houses where the workers live, a few peach trees, a church with two colored windows, and a miserable main street only a hundred yards long. On Saturdays the tenants from the near-by farms come in for a day of talk and trade. Otherwise the town is lonesome, sad, and like a place that is far off and estranged from all other places in the world. The nearest train stop is Society City, and

the Greyhound and White Bus Lines use the Fork Falls Road which
is three miles away. The winters here are short and raw, the summers
white with glare and fiery hot.

If you walk along the main street on an August afternoon there is
nothing whatsoever to do. The largest building . . . is boarded up . . .
and . . . looks completely deserted. Nevertheless, on the second floor
there is one window which is not boarded; sometimes in the late
afternoon . . . a hand will slowly open the shutter and a face will
look down on the town . . . as likely as not there will not be another
soul to be seen along the   street. There August afternoons
when your shift is finished there is absolutely nothing to do; you
might as well walk down to the Fork Falls Road and listen to the
chain gang.

I have quoted a fairly long passage from the book because, it seems to me, the
effect of McCullers's prose is accumulative. She does not work in a series of
detached, glittering phrases as, say, Truman Capote does. Nor does she, imitating
Faulkner, write sentences that coil up snakelike and then strike, suddenly, before
the period. Her language is cool and lucid, almost classical in its precision, her
descriptions clipped and occasionally cryptic. A nuance in one place, a repetition
or a shading somewhere else: this is all she needs really because, like the painter
Edward Hopper, she tends to rely on the resonance given to a detail by its total
context—and to use concealment almost as a medium of communication. The
inertia, the desolation, and the brooding violence of the small-town South are
caught in images that are hermetic, despite their apparent candor, and in incidents brimming with undisclosed biography.

The act is performed so quietly that it may tend to go unnoticed: what
McCullers has created here, in effect, is a world where emotion and vision can
coalesce—in which, through the agency of her prose, her own particular sense
of life can be externalized. The town is no dream kingdom, that is clear enough.
It is anchored in this world, in a firm if understated way, by such details as the
references to the bus and train services and by an implicit understanding of its
economic function. But it is no ordinary place, either—the kind of town we
might easily come across in Georgia, in the South, or anywhere else. Why? Because, quite apart from establishing this anchorage, the writer has used every
means at her disposal to reorder, rearrange, and so metamorphose; in a way that
must be familiar to us by now, she has created another country out of her own
known home. In this respect, the anonymity of the prose ties in with the evasiveness of the narrator, the hermeticism of the imagery with the apparent emptiness
of the scene. For together they direct our attention to precisely the same subject;

a feeling of "lonesomeness" or loss seems to result from them all. This feeling, needless to say, is not imposed on the material: as other writers like Thomas Wolfe could testify, it is there in the Deep South already, waiting to be acknowledged. McCullers has, however, emphasized it almost to the exclusion of everything else and, in doing so, cleverly established a nexus, a point of connection between the geometry of her self and the geography of her childhood surroundings. Gently, she has nudged the regional landscape into the expression of a fresh mood.

McCullers's aims are, of course, not just personal. Quite apart from externalizing her own state she is trying also, through the medium of the South, to anatomize human nature, to chart, in her plan of her region, the coordinates of all our lives. And in order to make this clear she will occasionally punctuate her narrative with little explanatory passages, like the following, which suggest that, remembering her own doubts about the possibility of proper contact between man and man—and, perhaps, experiencing some misgivings about her oblique methods elsewhere—the author is afraid the reader will otherwise miss the point.

> There are the lover and the beloved, but these two come from different countries. Often the beloved is only a stimulus for all the stored-up love which has lain quiet within the lover for a long time hitherto. And somehow every lover knows this. He feels in his soul that his love is a solitary thing. He comes to know a new, strange loneliness. . . . So there is only one thing for the lover to do. He must house his love within himself . . . ; he must create for himself a whole new inward world—a world intense and strange, complete in itself.

The longing to communicate and the difficulty of ever properly communicating, the delusions attendant upon the human need to love: the themes could hardly be presented more explicitly than they are here (indeed, the existence of a triangular relationship between personal feeling, regional landscape, and moral reference is virtually insisted upon) and this does, naturally, tend to carry its own dangers with it. The "message" may, as a result, seem a little too pat to be convincing, too limited and limiting even for the purpose of fable. The writer may, in short, end up with didacticism of the crudest possible kind. McCullers is saved from such dangers most of the time, I think, though; and what saves her more than anything else is her constant awareness of the *human* situation—the specifically emotional and imaginative terms into which her ideas have to be translated. Her landscapes, for all their initial sparseness, *are* inhabited. More to the point, the figures inhabiting them possess a special kind of resonance, that sense of roots and a definite history which marks them out as the descendants of recognizable southern types. They have the substance and immediate credibility of people long brooded over, and so well understood—and to this is added that freshness, the sense of surprise and valuable discovery, which can only come when someone as well known as this is seen from a radically altered standpoint. We may suspect, while we read a McCullers story, that we have seen characters like hers before; in fact, if we have read much earlier southern fiction we are sure we have. But until now, she makes us feel, we have never been properly acquainted with them: there is something about them, some crucial side of them we have somehow managed to miss.

The major characters in *The Ballad of the Sad Café* offer a perfect illustration of this, the way in which the familiar is suddenly turned into the strange and new. And the nature of their *familiarity*, at least, is suggested by a bare summary of the *Ballad*'s plot, which is like something borrowed from the comic legends of the old Southwest. There is a kind of crazy, comic logic of frustration behind everything that happens: the beloved is always turning away from the lover to create a false idol of his or her own. So "Miss Amelia" Evans, the central character and the owner of the "terrible, dim" face which appears in the opening portrait of the town, refuses the love of her husband, Marvin Macey, and, having done so, falls in love with a newcomer to the district, the hunchback "Cousin" Lymon. Cousin Lymon, in turn, despises Miss Amelia and worships Marvin Macey—who despises *him*. Nobody gets what he wants in the story. Everybody is thwarted and, in the process, made to look utterly grotesque. This, for example, is how Miss Amelia is described before the charade has properly begun:

> She was a dark, tall woman with bones and muscles like a man. Her hair was cut short and brushed back from the forehead, and there was about her sunburned face a tense, haggard quality. She might have been a handsome woman if, even then, she was not slightly cross-eyed.

By reducing her appearance to a series of conflicting angles, by emphasizing her physical defects and her masculinity (or, rather, her sexual ambivalence), McCullers effectively transforms Miss Amelia into a freak here—as much of a caricature in her own way as Sut Lovingood is, say, or any of the subhumans populating *Tobacco Road*. At least one of the strategies for presenting the character to us, in other words, seems to have been learned from Longstreet, Harris, and their imitators: we are distanced from Miss Amelia, made to inspect her and her country home with a clinical detachment, and then invited to consider her frustrations, such as they are—her utter failure to realize her ambitions in her given world—as at the very least potentially comic. As if to confirm McCullers's debt, there is even an epic fight at the end of the *Ballad*, between Miss Amelia and

Marvin Macey, which in its combination of the macabre and the grotesque (Macey greases himself, for instance, so that he can keep slipping through Miss Amelia's fingers) must remind us of those almost operatic trials of strength which enliven so many of the tales of the southwestern school.

That is not the whole story, though. If it were, we could hardly talk about McCullers making her characters new. Miss Amelia is a grotesque, perhaps, but she is a grotesque for the same reason that most of McCullers's subjects are— because, as the author herself once put it, her "physical incapacity" is being used primarily as "a symbol of [her] spiritual incapacity . . . —[her] spiritual isolation." She is not just the comic loser, nor is she economically deprived in the way that Jeeter Lester and Ty Ty Walden are. She is, to use that word again, "lonesome," and her lonesomeness is intended eventually to figure our own. Like an image seen in a carnival mirror, she is meant to offer us an exaggerated, comically distorted, and yet somehow sadly accurate reflection of ourselves. Exactly what this means, in terms of the total effect she has upon us, will perhaps become clear if we look at the way she is described toward the end of the story, when both Marvin Macey and Cousin Lymon have deserted her.

> Miss Amelia let her hair grow ragged, and it was turning grey. Her face lengthened, and the great muscles of her body shrank until she was thin as old maids are thin when they go crazy. And those grey eyes—slowly day by day they were more crossed, . . . as though they sought each other out to exchange a little glance of grief and lonely recognition.

This, surely, is to give the familiar caricature a fresh dimension. The details of Miss Amelia's appearance are just as grotesque as they ever were, but they appear to be placed now in a changed, and more sympathetic, context. We are drawn to the woman even while she still seems a little odd to us. The knowledge we have of her by this time has, of course, something to do with this development: we understand why she is odd and, understanding, we perhaps suspect that her oddity touches upon ours. And certain fragments of descriptive detail, which hint at pity as much as ridicule, are possibly relevant as well—the comparison with "crazy" old maids, for example, or the partly funny, partly moving account that McCullers now gives us of Miss Amelia's crossed eyes. But of immeasurably more significance than either of these things, I think, is something almost indefinable—which, for want of a better phrase, we must call the sheer texture of her prose. It goes back, in fact, to what I was saying earlier about McCullers's style, that it manages to be lyrical and colloquial, lucid and enigmatic, at one and the same time. For it is as a direct consequence of this strange combination, really, that we find ourselves held back from Miss Amelia here—and brought close up into a special kind of intimacy with her as well. She is distanced from us by a certain lingering freakishness of expression, a mysterious image, it may be, or a quirky turn of phrase; and yet she is also brought into an immediate contact with us by our sense that this is, after all, a conventional idiom we are listening to—that the language Miss Amelia inhabits, so to speak, belongs to normal, everyday conversation. This is an extraordinarily subtle relationship to set up between character and reader—far subtler than anything we are likely to come across elsewhere, in the work of other writers who have experimented with the southern comic mode. It has its origins, of course, in McCullers's belief that a paradox lurks at the heart of experience, naturally attaching itself to the idea of a *shared* isolation. As for its issue, that we find in the mood or *ambiance* to which our minds first return when recalling a McCullers novel—our memories of a quiet, but peculiarly inclusive, pathos.

Pathos; it is an unfashionable term partly because, through bad use, it has acquired an odor of sentimentality—become associated with what Ezra Pound once called that most inhumane of emotions, an indiscriminate sympathy. The unlucky man wallowing in his own bad luck, the account of poverty or suffering that begins and ends in moral posturing, without any reference being made to the possible agencies of change: these are the sort of things to which we tend to apply the word "pathetic" now. Nor are matters helped much, I suppose, by the memories most of us have of films that have been described as pathetic—where, more often than not, a patently contrived series of events is used as a pretext for self-indulgence. Pathos, in such cases, becomes the emotional equivalent of beating one's head against the wall—an exquisitely painful way of preparing for the moment when the pain stops, and the release offered by the inevitable happy ending arrives. Still, there is no reason why misuse of a word should blind us to its proper uses; and I would like to suggest that McCullers's fiction, at its best (by which I mean *The Ballad of the Sad Café*, *The Member of the Wedding*, and parts of *The Heart is a Lonely Hunter*), can supply us with a valuable corrective to all this. For it shows, I think, how tough and really critical an emotion pathos can be. Her characters are pathetic, but they are pathetic in the finest sense—in the same way that, to continue an earlier analogy, a good Chaplin film is. That is to say, the melancholy we experience while contemplating Miss Amelia Evans or Frankie Addams in *The Member of the Wedding* stems principally from the shock of recognition, our feeling that part of our own lives has been accurately defined. It encourages us not to escape from problems, still less to accept them, but simply to become more aware—to understand, fully to understand, their general scope. In this way the pathetic is used as an agent of moral instruction more than anything else, a means of telling us, quietly and sadly, what we are and the most we can do and of advising us, by inference, as to how we should behave.

McCullers's is, then, the definitive use of a specific emotional effect—a pathos that at once lends a strange atmosphere to landscape and character, and helps establish an intimate, unusually searching relationship between tale and reader. This is an impressive achievement—showing the kind of subtlety and even deviousness of intent we are perhaps more inclined to associate with more "difficult" fiction—and its very impressiveness has, I believe, led one or two of McCullers's critics into overestimating her. For there is a tendency, noticeable especially among those with a bias toward the New Criticism, to assume that because her work represents a perfect adaptation of means to ends she is, therefore, more or less unsurpassed among writers of her own region. So Walter Allen, in his standard history of the modern English and American novel, places her second only to Faulkner; and Gore Vidal, going one characteristic step further than this, insists, "of all our southern writers Carson McCullers is the one most likely to endure." Such commentary, I think, is exaggerated and unhelpful: the very perfection of McCullers's work depends, after all, upon her own level-headed acceptance of her limitations. She knows that she can describe, quite subtly, one particular dilemma or area of life and she concentrates almost her entire resources on that. There is no place in her fiction, really, for the rich "over-plus" of experience—by which I mean any aspects of behavior that cannot be included under the heading of theme, or any dimensions of feeling that cannot be reconciled with the major effect of pathos. And recognizing this she demonstrates little interest in such matters as the historical and social context, and no commitment either to the idea of a developing consciousness. Her people walk around and around within the circle of their own personalities, their inner world of thought and desire hardly engaging with the outer world at all. They seldom change, except physically, they never reflect more than one aspect of our experience (admittedly, it is a significant one); and to inflate them, their world, or indeed their creator to a major status—to suppose, in fact, that McCullers's novels and short stories are any more important to the tradition than they genuinely are—is, I believe, to be guilty of what used to be called "overkill." It is, in other words, to smother a quiet but effective talent by heaping upon it unearned and patently unacceptable praise.

As for McCullers's actual achievement, though, setting aside all such exaggeration, that surely is certain and secure. She is not a major writer, despite anything that Allen, Vidal, or any other critic may say to the contrary. But she is a very good minor one—so good, indeed, that she seems to reap a definite advantage from her minor status and turn her limitations into virtues. The absence of the historical dimension is a useful illustration of this. With many other writers, and especially southern ones, such an absence might prove fatal—indeed it *has* proved fatal, I think, in the case of Tennessee Williams and the earlier Capote. With McCullers, however, just the opposite is true; and this because in some strange way she manages to make history function as an *absent presence* in her work. It seems to be not so much omitted from her writing as concealed, made to disappear, and in such a way that the disappearance itself, like the disappearance of the religious perspective from later Victorian fiction, encourages our active comment. McCullers's characters, we infer, have not even this, the mere possibility of a tradition, to sustain them; they can only hang as Lowell's Czar Lepke does, "oas[es] in . . . [the] air/of lost connections"—so disoriented as to have no point of reference really, no common denominator with which to chart their disorientation. They may suffer pangs of nostalgia; in fact most of them do, it is a natural consequence of their loneliness. But that nostalgia is for a condition they can hardly define. They may be adrift, homesick; but that homesickness is for a place that has never, personally, been theirs. Just as space seems to recede from them even while it is being described, to try to hide from them in a way, so time in its larger dimension appears somehow to mock them by remaining hidden; the vacuum its departure creates is, we sense, *there* as a positive force in the narrative contributing to their despair. One sometimes wonders if, in all this, McCullers is not trying to add her own idiosyncratic footnote to Nietzsche by suggesting that not only God, that traditional comforter of the lonely and spiritually disfigured, is dead now—history, as a common secular resource and the modern substitute for God, is as well.

MARGARET B. McDOWELL

Short Stories and Poems

I. STORIES OF CHILDHOOD AND ADOLESCENCE

A half-dozen of McCullers's published stories focus on a child or adolescent—of these, the most impressive attainment is "Wunderkind," her first published work, written when she was only fifteen, and "Correspondence," written in 1941, about the time of *The Ballad of the Sad Café*. While the six stories vary considerably in form and quality, McCullers analyzes in each the situation of a child caught in a difficult position and reacting to it with bewilderment and frustration. In each, the point of view is so clearly defined that the reader identifies completely with the child who is coping with the complexities both of his or her situation and the complexities of his or her own development as an individual.

One early sketch, "Breath from the Sky," commands attention for its presentation of a dying child entirely from that child's point of view and for its realism. The child is neither one who rejoices to see the gates of heaven opening nor one who blesses the family from whom she is departing. Constance, who appears to be dying of tuberculosis, feels that she is about to be abandoned by her family—and even by her hated, domineering nurse—as they prepare her for her trip to a rest home. Reclining in a chair on the lawn, she envies her family as they leave to go swimming, and she longs to be washed by the blue lake and to suck the blue sky into herself in order to make the color a part of her, thereby enlivening the dull gray of her existence. Unused to being out-of-doors, she

From *Carson McCullers*. © 1980 by Twayne Publishers. Originally entitled "Short Stories, Poems, and a Second Play."

focuses today on a blade of grass as she suffers a fit of coughing, because she has been used to focus on a crack in the floor in her room when she was caught by the coughing fits. She longs also for the freshness of the sky, in order to escape the contamination she associates with her illness and which, she thinks, makes others reject her.

She is completely isolated and frustrated, because she feels that no one truly can sympathize with her. The efficient and cold nurse gives her admonitions about the value of cheerfulness. Her mother also makes every effort to appear unemotional, probably to keep from showing the child her own grief. Her voice is "brittle," and as she leaves, an almost imperceptible shudder passes across her shoulders. Constance interprets her mother's evasiveness as a rejection of her because of her "dirtiness."

Exhausted and loathing herself, Constance forces her mother to cut her long hair. So great is her sense of contamination that she will not let her sister even use the pile of hair to make a pillow for the dog. She tries not to spit out the thick strands of phlegm that drain from her lungs as she coughs. This central scene in which Constance demands that her hair be cut in an effort to be cleansed and accepted, becomes more poignant as one recognizes the energy with which the mother hacks at the girl's hair, as if determined to cut herself away from the child who must leave the next day—and possibly forever. Her hurrying away to take the rest of the family swimming may also suggest a determination on her part to keep the rest of the family involved in the satisfying routines related to life rather than death. The tension created by the mother's brittle voice and hurried movements and by the nurse's exaggerated cheeriness provides an ironic background for the child's thoughts about abandonment.

McCullers's portrayal contrasts with that of the archetypally innocent and serene dying child, so common in literature of the past and reaching its apogee in the death of Little Nell in Dickens's *The Old Curiosity Shop*, of Little Eva in Harriet Beecher Stowe's *Uncle Tom's Cabin*, and of Helen Burns in Charlotte Brontë's *Jane Eyre*. The use of the child's point of view, the realistic depiction of the ugliness of her disease, and the petulance, weariness, and self-loathing of the patient sweep aside any trace of sentimentality that one might associate with the death of a young person. Subtly, McCullers blends the child's longing to be clean and lovable with her disappointment in missing a chance to go swimming with the rest of the family. Because she writes from the child's perspective, McCullers convinces the reader that staying home from the swimming expedition and being sent away from her mother is worse than facing imminent death.

The forceful evocation of situation in this sketch elicits sympathy for the victim, although she is still a repugnant child and her disease is loathsome.

Though it contains an arresting portrayal, "Breath from the Sky" is essentially static. It is a vignette, rather than a story in which the structure is well defined, in which tensions develop between individuals, and in which a character changes significantly. It is prophetic, however, in the sense that McCullers would actually become a distinguished creator of character, particularly of children.

In a more extended and dynamic portrayal of a troubled child, "The Haunted Boy" (1955), McCullers explores the trauma of ten-year-old Hugh, who returns from school to find his mother absent and then relives the experience which he has tried to forget. The previous year he had discovered his mother's bleeding body after she had attempted suicide, and he and his father had had to live alone for months after the mother was hospitalized. When Hugh's affectionate and lighthearted mother returns in an hour or so from her first shopping spree since her recovery, Hugh bitterly turns on her and tells her she looks too old for the frivolous dress and slippers she has bought. Through the reliving of his horror, through his expression of anger at his mother's willingness to abandon him and his father, and through the reassurance which both parents can now give him, Hugh by the end of the story gains a measure of peace. This work illustrates the psychic tension of a child torn between pity for—and anger against—a parent and also the tension between his need to appear mature and his need to express his fear. Most effective is the dramatic irony implicit in his sudden abusive anger at the very moment that he experiences relief at his mother's return.

In four other stories about young people, dramatic tension develops as each protagonist matures as a result of difficult and harrowing experience. "Sucker," "Like That," and "Wunderkind" preceded all of the novels; "Correspondence" followed The Ballad of the Sad Café in 1941. Primary interest in "Sucker" and "Like That" lies in their relation to McCullers's early development as artist, particularly her ability to depict character and her use of themes related to love and to the acquiring of self-knowledge. But "Wunderkind" and "Correspondence" deserve attention for their merit apart from their position in McCullers's canon.

In both "Sucker" and "Like That" McCullers analyzes parallel crises in the lives of two young siblings. The narrators, who are also the protagonists, plan simply to report facts about a brother or sister, but actually talk more about changes that have occurred in themselves as a formerly close relationship with a brother or sister has diminished. In "Sucker," sixteen-year-old Pete recounts how his twelve-year-old foster-brother has changed his name from "Sucker" to "Richard" after Pete one night, frustrated by Maybelle, his first love, angrily turned against Sucker. In "Like That" a thirteen-year-old talks about her older sister's preoccupation during the last several months with whatever had happened on "a certain night this summer" when she had stayed out late with a college student. In "Like That" the narrator is given no name and the sister is only called "Sis," perhaps to emphasize their representativeness as adolescents more than their individuality.

Pete's impatience with Sucker, followed by his remorse, anticipates Frankie Addams's ambivalent behavior toward little John Henry in *The Member of the Wedding*, as she alternately avoids him and then seeks his companionship; it also anticipates Mick Kelly's regret in *The Heart Is a Lonely Hunter* when Bubber changes his name to "George," becomes a "tough kid," and takes his best marbles out of their hiding place in her mattress.

Both protagonists communicate the satisfaction that they had experienced in the old days of spontaneous comradeship and recreate vividly the single eventful night that changed their relationship. For Pete, his guilt at hurting Sucker adds to the grief related to the child's separation from him. So does his chagrin when he realizes that loss of Sucker's admiration overshadows the frustration which he had felt over Maybelle's rejection of him, the event that led to the attack on Sucker. In "Like That," the narrator's bewilderment, her fears about her elder sister, and her apprehension that this same mysterious trouble may be her own fate in a few years' time deepen her sense of isolation and the pain of the psychic distance which now separates her from her sister.

Unfortunately, McCullers's effort in both of these stories to imitate the spontaneous language of the child or the adolescent results in looseness of organization, relatively unconnected expressions of emotion, and the inclusion of irrelevant details. She had not yet developed the control of language and of action which she manifested in her novels and in some of her short stories. McCullers used first-person narration only one other time in her later fiction—in "Correspondence," in which the epistolary convention provides a degree of stylistic control. Her necessary mastery of the formal aspects of her artistry can be associated, in part, perhaps, with her abandonment of the first-person point of view and her subsequent use of an omniscient narrator.

In the better, though extremely early, "Wunderkind," McCullers demonstrates her ability to write with a more compressed and forceful style than she used in "Sucker" or "Like That." She reveals far greater control, directness, and economy in her depiction of fifteen-year-old Frances, who hopes to become a great pianist and who had, several years before, been hailed as a "wunderkind" by the crotchety Mr. Bilderbach, her teacher. With no children of his own, he has projected his feeling toward her and has become for her a second father, just as his wife has become a mother of sorts to Frances, making her junior high graduation dress, for example, and providing milk and cookies when she comes twice a week for her lessons. For four months Frances has been discouraged because she cannot actualize the music that she hears in her mind and feels in her

heart, although she has attained technical competence in the difficult composi-
tions which she practices for hours each day. She does not understand the dis-
crepancy between the music she hears in her mind and the music that she elicits
from the piano, but she knows that she cannot stand the strain of this conflict
much longer. All that seems real to her now is the music she hears in her mind
and cannot duplicate when she sits down to play.

All the action, the dialogue—and most importantly, the music—filter
through Frances's memory and reflect her anxiety. The story builds quickly to a
climax and almost immediately ends. Frances arrives for the lesson late in the
winter afternoon at the downtown Cincinnati apartment and rushes out a short
time later as the story closes. Except for a brief encounter with the violinist who
teaches Heime (another wunderkind), only Frances and Bilderbach appear.

A maze of paradoxes surrounds Frances. The story would be far simpler—
and less effective—if Bilderbach (or the more successful Heime) were her antagonist and she could direct her anger at him. Instead, the music, which is her
greatest love, is also her antagonist. The music exists as part of herself, as well as
an outside force to deal with. Bilderbach, though her judge on this crucial occasion, is also the only comrade she could depend on in her struggle with her overwhelming challenger. But even his comprehension of her situation is limited, and
he also suffers from Frances's sense of defeat by music. She cannot return to the
vigorous proficiency she had enjoyed in childhood any more than she can advance
to the level of genius predicted by her teacher when she was only twelve. (When
Bilderbach, seeing the tears in her eyes, suggests she play a simple composition
she knew three years before, she refuses.) Frances's abandoning of her music is
not an impulsive yielding to discouragement, but rather an act of courage, because it represents her acknowledgment that a part of herself has died. As she
leaves her teacher's apartment, music has vanished from the silent room and from
her as a creative artist. Bilderbach stands mute, with hands relaxed and hanging
at his side; and the door shuts firmly behind her. Every detail implies finality,
that an essential part of Frances's self has gone.

The ending may suggest Frances's maturing—her realistic judgment of her
ability and her facing of herself as a human being who struggles and still fails.
More poignantly, however, the ending is devastating for Frances. Having made
her decision after months of agonizing over her dilemma, she enjoys no elation or
even relief. She stumbles, she drags her heavy books, and, once outside, she,
ominously, turns in the wrong direction. The street's noise and confusion assail
her senses. Ironically, the noise and confusion that intensify her suffering as she
rushes down the street come from those happy children, who were never destined
to be wonderful. She has lost her music and her special friends; beyond this, she
realizes now that she earlier had lost irretrievably her life as an ordinary child, a

life marked by noise, confusion, and laughter—and until now, she did not know that the loss of such experience mattered at all.

Though McCullers uses an impersonal narrative voice, she skillfully adapts the narrative passages to the child's feelings, particularly as Frances waits for her lesson to begin. She examines the picture of Heime on the cover of a music magazine and realizes that, though he has been the only child she has had time to associate with for three years because of her hours of practice, she actually does not know what he looks like. She knows exactly what his fingers look like when she performs at concerts with him, and she knows exactly what he smells like as he stands beside the piano. One recognizes from her thoughts on Heime the utter impersonality that has narrowed her life to a preoccupation with his fingers and with her own. She dismisses Heime from her mind with the thought: "Heime always seemed to smell of corduroy pants and the food he had eaten and rosin." As she looks at his picture, it occurs to her momentarily that "his finger looked as though it would pluck the wrong string." But Heime is a mere distraction; music itself is her problem.

If she does not know what Heime looks like, we never know what she looks like because her appearance does not matter to her. We know how she moves—dragging her satchel, stumbling clumsily, and feeling her arms weighted down by her books. Her hands are enemies beyond her control: they fumble as she pulls out her music; her fingers twitch and her tendons quiver as she recalls her morning's practice; and she observes that the adhesive bandage on her sore finger is dirty and curling. As if the music she hears in her mind is the reality and what she actually hears is unreal because it is wrong, she looks intently at her fingers almost to reassure herself that they are part of her.

McCullers vividly creates the setting, the people, and the details found in the story, although we know Mrs. Bilderbach; Mr. Lafkowitz, the violin teacher; and Heime only through Frances's thoughts. The dialogue is sparse, occurring only at the most crucial points. When she finishes playing, for example, Mr. Bilderbach says only one word: "No." The single word changes her life. The precision and sensitivity revealed in this story, McCullers's first published work, provided sure evidence of her talent even before she left the South for New York.

In autumn 1941 McCullers wrote "Correspondence," an epistolary sketch in the voice of still another adolescent, fourteen-year-old Henrietta (Henky) Evans, who changes from an open and trusting young girl to a disappointed and cynical adult in her two and a half months of letter-writing to a South American boy who never answers, though he volunteered in a magazine to be a pen-pal. Henky declares, "Recently I have thought a whole lot about life. I have pondered over a great many things such as why we were put on the earth. I have decided that I do not believe in God. On the other hand, I am not an atheist." Her letters suggest the one poignant truth about growing up—the attenuation of spontaneous emotion. Mistrust and suspicion in McCullers's work often mark the transition from childhood trustfulness to youthful experience. So in this story a guarded formality and a mere polite expression of disapproval replace in the fourth letter the appealing spontaneity of the first.

McCullers's artistic excellence may be most notable here in the subtlety with which she conveys what Henky herself does not realize—her self-centeredness. Though angry at Manoel's disinterest in her, she does not in her writing reach out to learn about a culture far different from her own. She remarks that she has always been "crazy about" South Americans, but has never met one. She would be disturbed if Manoel wrote and talked of himself and his land, rather than reacting to her letters. She seeks a mirror image of herself in another hemisphere, just as the narcissistic characters in *The Heart Is a Lonely Hunter* talk to Singer, who seems to them to understand perfectly, although he, like Manoel, never answers. It is as if she writes the letters to herself, a kind of talking aloud.

Although her conclusions are pompous, Henky engagingly in the first letter acknowledges some of her shortcomings. She wants to be a tragic actress, but her performance in a recent play failed. Another failure, which anticipates the anxiety of Frankie Addams in *The Member of the Wedding*, lies in her inability to be "exactly like the other freshmen." She closes her first letter with the hope that Manoel's letter will arrive soon—to reassure her that he is the spiritual twin she seeks: "I am looking forward exceedingly to hearing from you and find out if I am right about our feeling so much alike about life and other things. You can write to me anything that you want to, as I have said before that I feel I already know you so well."

The themes developed in Henky's letters are those encountered elsewhere in McCullers's fiction: the essential narcissism of human beings, the longing for reciprocity in any expression of interest or affection, and the ironic combination of gain and loss as one grows up. The sketch, however, deserves attention apart from its relationship to McCullers's explorations of these themes in her longer works. The humor in the treatment of the child is incisive, but McCullers tempers her satire of Henky's failure to recognize her self-centeredness with just the appropriate balance of the ironic and of good-natured tolerance.

II. HUMOR IN THE SHORT STORIES

Besides "Correspondence," several other excellent stories reveal McCullers's satirical humor. Notable in her early work is the brief, single-scene story "The Jockey" (1941), which excels by virtue of its sustained tension between strong emotion and its repression. The whole situation explodes as emotions are let loose in the violent closing of the story. The story appeared in the *New Yorker* a month after McCullers completed it at Yaddo, just two miles from the Saratoga hotel where it is laid.

Against an elegant background in the hotel dining room, three rich men who derive fortunes from the racetrack sit stuffing themselves with rich food and drink. All regard the jockeys, who make their fortunes possible by risking their lives in the races, as less than human. They speak derisively of an older jockey, Bitsy Barlow, who has been "strange" ever since "his Irish friend" was killed three years before. Bitsy, they claim, has gained three pounds and still was seen eating a lamb chop.

Barlow enters the room. A tiny man, he exaggerates his impeccable manners with a haughty theatricality. He stands beside their table, condescendingly looking down on the men who figuratively look down on him and the other jockeys. With perfect control of his anger, he tells them the news of his young friend, injured months ago, whose cast was removed that morning and whose leg had shrunk. The three rich men remain unmoved by the news. With great aplomb, Bitsy astonishes them by deliberately removing two french fries from a plate, chewing them, and then spitting the food on the beautiful rug. He cries out loudly, "Libertines!" Immediately, he resumes his dignified bearing and marches rigidly from the room, leaving the startled trio to be humiliated by the curiosity and laughter of the other patrons in the dining room.

As memorable as the explosive climax is the hypnotic effect built from the beginning of the story by Barlow's cold and controlled hostility toward the three men, which continues to intensify until the moment of attack. Memorable also is the stylized artifice that balances the stereotypical rich men against the tiny figure who reveals compassion for the exploited and who protests against their exploitation. McCullers treats the three "libertines" only half-seriously, because they must not become fully human or appear as even an interesting subspecies. They must remain stereotypes, designated at first as the bookie, the trainer, and the rich man, and somewhat later merely as Sylvester, Simmons, and Seltzer.

The dramatic impact of the story largely derives from the contrast between Barlow's apparently impulsive act and the pride and dignity, the extreme restraint and propriety, and the precision and deliberateness which he has shown to the final moment. Impulse has no place in his world, where he must calculate each motion in order to pare from his time the few seconds by which he can set a new record in a race. McCullers also uses many details metaphorically to emphasize Barlow's characteristic rigidity: his heels bite sharply into the deep rug as he marches into the dining room; he bows stiffly; he combs his hair in a stiff band; he wears a "precisely" tailored suit; he opens his cigarette box with a definite snap; he sharply clinks his bracelet on the table; and he drinks his whiskey "neat in two hard swallows."

One might at first see Bitsy Barlow as a tiny man related to the dwarfs which McCullers used in her slightly earlier *Reflections in a Golden Eye* and *The Ballad of the Sad Café*, but he has nothing in common with Anacleto or Cousin Lymon, except diminished physical stature. Certainly he would refuse ever to allow himself to be seen as freakish or childlike.

"Madame Zilensky and the King of Finland" (1941), along with "The Jockey" and "The Sojourner" (1951), best exemplifies McCullers's ability to combine humor and pathos in the portrayal of characters who are likable but whose weaknesses make them vulnerable and who provide her with subjects for a mildly satirical art. In this story McCullers uses only two characters, both music professors at a small college, Mr. Brook and Madame Zilensky; and she explores with both delicacy and a sardonic mockery the relationship which develops between them. The rather colorless Brook, described as "a somewhat pastel" figure, has spent his life with Mozart minuets and "explanations about diminished sevenths and minor triads." Madame Zilensky, his colleague-to-be, arrives from Europe with her three little boys to take over her new post, and a far from placid existence results for him as he gradually discovers that she embodies many of his own repressed impulses and aspirations. If Brook lectures quietly on musical theory, composition, and Mozart, the more inspired and imaginative Madame Zilensky teaches with dramatic force and fitful energy. Soon after her arrival, she finds four pianos for her studio and loses no time in setting "four dazed students to playing Bach fugues together. The racket that came from her end of the department was extraordinary."

McCullers develops a complex pattern of contrasts between Brook and Madame Zilensky, and from these contrasts the organization of the story emerges. Harmony, as well as dissonance, characterizes their friendship. Mr. Brook's appreciation for "counterpoint" in musical composition relates metaphorically to his secret enjoyment of Madame Zilensky's departures from conventionality, logic, and quiet routine into a more zestful and creative world so different from his own conventional one. One also gradually recognizes that, while Brook and Madame Zilensky contrast with each other, each also possesses in his own right a kind of divided spirit, living a life that others see but also another life—secret, imaginative, and satisfying—which others are blind to or else see only intermittently. Mr. Brook can understand Madame Zilensky only because he himself lives a double life and achieves self-realization only in his fantasy world.

Madame Zilensky puzzles, exasperates, and fascinates Mr. Brook by the paradoxical nature of her personality and interests. She works to the point of exhaustion on what Brook considers her twelve "immense and beautiful" symphonies, but the next morning she remarks to him about the delightful evening she spent at a card party. His eyes light up a little when he listens to her oblique references to her adventures, world travels, lovers, and famous friends. She believes the fantasies that she reports—if only for the moment. For example, though all of her little boys look alike, she tells Brook one day about the father of each, all the time "thinking hard." Boris's father, she invents with a dreamy smile, was a Pole who played a piccolo. The father of Sammy, with whom she enjoys less rapport, was "that French," she declares indignantly, the man who probably still possesses her lost metronome. The absence of her metronome is the first thing that she mentions as she arrives on the train without her luggage in the opening of the story; and at various times, she becomes suddenly agitated about its disappearance, although she never replaces it. Curiously, Mr. Brook twice offers to give her his, but he never does; nor does she seem eager to acquire it. The metronome seems to symbolize the orderliness and conventionality lacking in her life of varying rhythms and imaginative elaborations. Her little boys also move to a rhythm of their own, as if in imitation of the idiosyncrasy of their mother. When they enter a room, they never step on the rug but carefully tiptoe around the edge of the room to keep their shoes on the floor.

Mr. Brook, on the other hand, is much more conventional and is more timid about giving actuality to his fantasies than is Madame Zilensky. He follows the rules of society and the regulations of his college, and he lives a life which is conscientious, orderly, and dull. But gradually his other life in the world of his imagination becomes dominant, and it draws him into Madame Zilensky's orbit and permits him to understand her—at least when he sits dozing by the fireside with a copy of Blake's poems and a glass of apricot brandy beside him and Mahler phrases drifting across his mind. Like Madame Zilensky, he is also a secret romantic and a psychic adventurer. When the music department had decided to "gang together" for a summer in Salzburg, Brook vanished and went alone to Peru—a gesture of self-assertion on his part and a rejection of the conventional expectations his colleagues have of him. In his brandied dreams, when his imagination soars, he identifies with Madame Zilensky's urge to invent the lies which "doubled the little of her existence that was left over from work" and allow her to expand the self to its greatest possible dimensions.

Since Brook is, however, the revolutionary in theory who does not have the courage of his revolutionary predispositions, one day he wakes up, brushes his teeth, polishes his spectacles, and decides to assert the orderly side of his life and by implication feels it necessary to curb the imaginative excesses of his colleague. He now sees it as his duty to confront "the pathological liar." The pain, which he sees etched in her face when he accuses her of lying, so alarms him that he immediately begins encouraging her to continue her fable about the king of Finland, a country which has no king. "And was he nice?" Brook asks.

The intricate elaboration of the contrasts within each of the two characters, the contrasts established between the two people, and the similarity of their desire to transcend a dull reality contribute to the involuted and convoluted comic effects generated in this story. These effects are subtle and inhere as much in the unobtrusive behavior and basic tolerance of Mr. Brook as in the zestful and flamboyant eccentricity of Madame Zilensky. The intricacy of McCullers's technique in the story and the depth of the psychological exploration to be found in it are suggested by her use of contrapuntal patterns through which parallel characters and situations develop simultaneously, as it were, and reflect implicitly upon one another; by the vital presence of the music of Mahler, Mozart, and Bach; and also by the metronome as a symbolic illumination of the characters' tightly regulated lives. This story is McCullers's most thoughtful comedy, although "The Sojourner" is not far behind.

With much less depth of characterization and fullness of organization, McCullers in "Art and Mr. Mahoney" (1949) again makes music the background for the action and the characters' development. Using her keen sense for detail in phrase and manners, she satirizes the snobbery of music lovers at a concert and a reception. They display this snobbery toward Mr. Mahoney when he disgraces himself and his wife by clapping too soon and too enthusiastically at a pause in the program. All avert their eyes, his wife sits rigid and tense through the rest of the concert, and because of her humiliation, she converses with no one at the reception. Mahoney decides finally that he had a right to clap at what he enjoyed. Although the sketch makes its point as a satire upon ceremonious manners, its chief interest lies in its exposing the pretenses of provincially minded, so-called promoters of culture.

III. "A TREE, A ROCK, A CLOUD"

After McCullers finished *The Ballad of the Sad Café*, she returned to Georgia late in 1941, to resume her difficult effort in balancing the "poetic and prosaic strands" in *The Bride*, which later became *The Member of the Wedding*. She had filed for divorce and was suffering severe psychic stress concerning her lost ability to pray and even to sign her name. At home in the South she was able to recover something of her shattered equilibrium. According to Virginia Spencer Carr, Carson gradually thought of her retreat to the quieter life of the South as comparable to Annemarie Clarac-Schwarzenbach's sojourn in Africa. Annemarie wrote her from there about the spiritual awakening she was experiencing in her primitive surroundings.

McCullers was intermittently writing poems during these years, and one of the outstanding short poems produced at this time was "The Twisted Trinity":

> There was a time when stone was stone
> When a face on the street was a finished face
> And a leaf, my soul, and God alone
> Made instant symmetry.
> Now all things fail, the trinity is twisted.
> Stone is not stone. And faces like the fractioned characters
> In dreams are incomplete.
> Until in the child's unfinished face I recognize
> Your sudden eyes.
> The soldier climbs the evening stair leaving
> Your shadow.
> And to the delicate autumn hill and the slant star
> The exiled intellect must add a new dimension:
> Something of you.

In October, Klaus Mann published "The Twisted Trinity" in *Decision*; in December, David Diamond produced a musical setting for it; and Annemarie wrote that she had translated it into German and that it had so inspired her that she attempted to write a similar poem.

In "The Twisted Trinity" the speaker avers that formerly her life had been spiritually integrated, and she had then perceived a clear relationship among self, nature, and God—an "instant symmetry." Now a new presence—that of a lover —has not only disturbed this harmony, but has deepened it, in providing a new dimension and mystery to experience. No longer is stone only stone, nor a face a "finished face," but stone and face acquire an infinitude of significance which they had never before possessed. Though a later version of this poem, published as "Stone Is Not Stone" (1947), is less positive and suggests the adverse effects of the lover's absence, it retains the central idea that love has changed the total perception of the speaker.

When she finally recovered from a two-month battle with pneumonia in late January 1942, Carson attempted to express in fiction the main theme of "The Twisted Trinity": for any individual, love transforms the perception of the self, nature, and God. But as her allegorical story "A Tree, a Rock, a Cloud" took shape, she created instead a tale based on the inversion of two of the concepts that inform the poem. If in the poem the lover's presence suggests the significance and mystery in the simple things that surround the poet, in the story it

is the beloved's desertion that makes the man frantic, driving him at first to
search for her and later to discover salvation through the "science of love," which
he has worked out in order to achieve a kind of spiritual therapy for his real
grief. If in the poem, it is love which is the transcendent aspects of nature, in
the story, McCullers reverses cause and effect, so that it is the close identification
with nature which enables the protagonist once again to attempt love and to gain
insight thereby into the transcendent aspects of sexual experience. By learning
to love one small object or living thing at a time, the man hopes that he will
eventually develop fully the ability to love a woman again, at least to love with
greater understanding than he had been able to do previously.

McCullers builds her story around a tramp's progressive experience as he
tries to put into practice his ideas concerning his newly formulated "science of
love." As he sips his beer at dawn in an all-night cafe, barely managing to keep
his big nose from dipping into the mug, he reminisces to a newsboy, whom he
has forced to listen to his tale. The protagonist searched for two years to recover
the wife who deserted him before he discovered his "science," which requires
that he try to experience feeling for a pet or an inanimate object, no matter how
repulsive, and then turn toward the expression of feeling for human beings. He
started with a goldfish, progressed to a stone, and now has travelled spiritually
far enough to tell the child that he loves him. Actually, however, after he tells his
tale, he shuffles away from the child without further thought of him; and the
child simply shrugs, with some embarrassment, and comments to Leo, the cynical
bartender, "He sure has done a lot of traveling." The encounter provides no indi-
cation that the tramp has learned to love, to see the need for commitment to
another person, or to inspire love.

Though McCullers often employed metaphor and used allegorical characters and situations in her longer fiction, this story stands alone among her short
stories in its use of abstract figures and its focus on a fable with a directly stated
philosophical message. Because the emphasis of the story is intellectual and abstract, the two main characters are deliberately left without names. They exist
metaphorically simply as "the boy" and as "the man" or "the tramp." In certain
other respects, however, the story illustrates some dominating characteristics of
nearly all her short fiction, with its focus on only two or three characters, its
brevity, its confinement to one problem or theme, its short time period, and its
setting in one small room. Although some critics have praised it highly—even, in
fact, regarding it as her best story—it remains, for me, too static to be among
her finest narratives. Most importantly, perhaps, McCullers's attempt to convert
a poem into a story represents from the first her versatility in experimentation
with a variety of genres and patterns. The illumination this story gives to "The
Twisted Trinity" and "Stone Is Not Stone" reflects her refusal ever to recognize

a rigid demarcation between poetry and fiction. It also relates clearly to her effort at this time to attain in *The Bride* an intricate interweaving and balance of the poetic and prosaic.

IV. THE ELUSIVENESS OF MARITAL OR FAMILY SECURITY

McCullers in nearly all of her short stories, as in her long works, places her central characters within family groups. Most often, the family establishes a stable or permanent background against which the crisis affecting the single character is developed. In certain other works, however, like "The Haunted Boy," an individual's crisis derives directly from the family's crisis.

Three of the short stories reflect the situation of the family plagued by alcoholism: "The Instant of the Hour After," which preceded the marriage of Carson and Reeves McCullers, although it seems almost prophetic of their troubled relationship; "Who Has Seen the Wind?" (1956), in which alcoholism appears to be both cause and effect of the protagonist's "writer's block"; and "A Domestic Dilemma" (1951), in which the alcoholic is a young housewife and mother, who is distressed by the move from her small southern town to a New York suburb, where she is isolated with small children.

"The Instant of the Hour After" is an exposé of the futility involved in the shiftless lives of alcoholics. After a guest leaves, the husband and wife argue derisively and interminably. The wife, who has recently decreased her own heavy drinking, has had during the evening a nightmarish glimpse of herself and her husband caught in a bottle, trying to climb up the glass wall, and failing. By the end of the evening, she feels contempt for her husband's arrogance and his insults directed toward the guest and herself, but she also feels anxiety and pity for him as he sits shaking with chills.

"Who Has Seen the Wind?" presents a similar couple and situation, although it is developed in several scenes—one revealing the alcoholic Ken's inability to continue his work as a fiction writer, another showing his contentiousness and insecurity in social situations, and still another, a crucial scene in which he shows his antagonism toward Marian, his wife, who has stopped drinking the previous year in alarm at the increasing violence of their quarrels. In this scene he is angered at her refusal to drink with him, and almost stabs and rapes her, but finally he lacks energy to express his hostility with overt violence and does not notice when she slips away. In a kind of postlude, the next day Ken wanders in the blinding snowdrifts toward certain suicide. The story reflects McCullers's lack of sure conception and organization in this rewritten version of a draft originally intended for the play *The Square Root of Wonderful*. Like the torment of the abusive and suicidal Phillip Lovejoy in that play, Ken's situation probably also reflects that of Reeves McCullers and, to some extent, that of Carson herself as a writer whose drinking seemed necessary to sustain her human relationships and even her writing, but which also interfered with them.

The first of these stories is an undeveloped sketch and the second, except for the violence of the final scene, is relatively monotonous in pace and disorganized; but both stories parallel, in the growing intensity of the woman's despair and in the mingled anger and compassion displayed for the alcoholic, the much more effective artistry of "A Domestic Dilemma" (1951). In this story McCullers attains greater depth in characterizing the individual caught between love and hate for a drunken spouse than in the other two tales, partly because Martin's characterization does not depend on a late-night harangue between two tired people, confused by alcohol. He arrives home from work, anxious about his children's safety, as he has been every day since Emily the year before dropped their baby on her head because she was too drunk to hold her. Martin's interaction is primarily with the children as he bathes and feeds them while his wife sleeps; the ambivalence of his feelings toward Emily gradually appears to the reader, though it is not evident to himself until the final moment of the story. As he bathes the children, he feels anger toward Emily for her inability to care for them and protect them, but as he feels tenderness for them when he bathes their bodies and when he watches them sleep, he finds waves of affection for Emily sweeping over him. When he is finally alone, fatigue, despair, and loathing for his wife overwhelm him. But again, as he prepares for bed, he looks at Emily, as he had gazed at the children in their sleep, and he is inexplicably drawn to her. Like the couple caught in the bottle in "The Instant of the Hour After," Martin sees himself and Emily caught together in bonds of suffering that are stronger than those of love, but those of love still survive. He slides into bed and reaches over, in his extreme weariness, simply to touch "the adjacent flesh," and life, for a moment, achieves again a glimmer of its lost radiance.

This story represents considerably greater artistry than that in either "The Instant of the Hour After" or "Who Has Seen the Wind?" particularly in its depiction of Martin's complex relationship with the other individuals—the children and Emily. The emphasis is only initially on Emily's drunkenness. The story also gains by McCullers's having extended her focus from Martin and his problems to those of Emily, though she appears directly in the story only for a few moments. She also suffers from the disharmony of the family situation. Her isolation, her homesickness for the South, and the guilt, anger, and love which she feels toward her children make her a considerable character, who finds a destructive release for unbearable tensions in her bouts of drinking. An irony exists in Martin's moments of great tenderness for his wife, experienced intermittently with his loathing for what she has become. It is as if he finds himself surprised that his love still exists and that there is still some urgency in his cherishing of her, since the bond between them has become so fragile. McCullers by this time in her career had gone beyond her early formulaic and quotable declarations in her fiction concerning the nature of love, deeply felt as they must sometimes have been. Love in this tale is a dominant and incomprehensible force, too complex to be separated from hatred, pity, memory, hope, or despair.

Like Martin in "A Domestic Dilemma," Ferris in "The Sojourner," another excellent story published only a few months earlier, reveals a man who is surprised by the strength of love and by his vulnerability with respect to it. Returning to Paris from his father's funeral in Atlanta, Ferris glimpses his former wife, Elizabeth, on the street in New York. Later, frustrated that he can reach no old friends by telephone, he impulsively calls her. That night as he briefly visits her home, she graciously serves him a surprise birthday cake, with thirty-eight candles, while he marvels that she looks like a Madonna with her children. He feels a tinge of jealousy for Elizabeth's new husband, a touch of anxiety about having lost his own youthful days, and a momentary grief—not just for his father's death but for the loss of his own family ties, which he had recognized in Atlanta the previous day and which he experiences again, and with greater intensity, with Elizabeth. He has been a sojourner—from the South, to New York, to Europe—and he has stopped only briefly in his journey for a few years of marriage. Mourning a death and celebrating a birthday so close together now ironically emphasize for Ferris the brevity of life, and he realizes he may be throwing away the best part of his own by being unable to commit himself to another person. The apparently idyllic life of Elizabeth's new family and the closeness of the family which he tried for a few days to rejoin in the South suggest to him that a sojourner who seeks the fullness of life by refusing to give up any of his freedom may, in actuality, miss the fullness of life. Back in Paris, he sits in the apartment of his sweetheart, Jeannine, waiting for her to return from the club where she sings and cuddling her lonely little son, whom he has previously tended to ignore.

But Ferris's new attempt to love is not at all selfless. He presses the child close in desperation as he feels "the terror, the acknowledgment of wasted years and death" and hopes that "an emotion as protean as his love could dominate the pulse of time." Ferris remains the type of the twentieth-century intellectual who is hedonistic, self-centered, and unable to learn from experience. One concludes that Ferris as sojourner may settle down to a committed love for Jeannine and Valentin, but that the roots he puts down may not be deep. He is so consistently treated with a touch of the satiric and the sardonic that one suspects that he will, in some sense, remain a sojourner in spite of the insights which his pilgrimage to his past has symbolically provided for him. Unfortunately, he may remain a person who accepts the momentary pleasure and the frustration of a man who is supposedly free but is in reality a hollow individual—a sojourner in this life, who evades its challenges and difficulties and so never achieves its rewards

McCullers's interest in experimenting with various styles and genres was again manifested as she adapted this story as a successful play for television. It appeared on the "Omnibus" series as "The Invisible Wall" on December 27, 1953.

V. POEMS

Apart from "The Twisted Trinity" (1941) all of McCullers's published poems appeared in the late 1940s and early 1950s, immediately after she had persevered so long and succeeded so well in attempting to blend poetry and prose in *The Member of the Wedding.* Even "The Twisted Trinity" was revised during this period and reprinted as "Stone Is Not Stone." This was the time in her career when she enjoyed her greatest acclaim, with the Broadway success of *The Member of the Wedding* and the publication of the omnibus volume in 1951, but it was also a time of great psychic and physical stress. Physicians were raising her hopes and then disappointing her with various explanations for her strokes and predictions about her chances to regain some physical agility and to lessen her constant pain. Her second marriage to Reeves and their ever-growing dependence on alcohol increased her suffering until the distress culminated in his suicide in 1953.

In 1950 and 1951 she composed her most ambitious work of poetry, a cycle of five poems, "The Dual Angel: A Meditation on Origin and Choice." Some of these poems she wrote while she was being entertained by famous writers—Elizabeth Bowen at the ancient Bowen's Court near Dublin in 1950, Dame Edith Sitwell in England in 1951, and Princess Marguerite Caetoni, editor of *Botteghe Oscure,* at her eleventh-century castle outside Rome in 1952. The cycle of poems, dedicated to Dame Edith Sitwell, appeared in 1952 in both *Botteghe Oscure* and *Mademoiselle.*

The five poems which comprise "The Dual Angel: A Meditation on Origin and Choice" range from ten to forty-seven lines: "Incantation to Lucifer," "Hymen, O Hymen," "Love and the Rind of Time," "The Dual Angel," and "Father, Upon Thy Image We Are Spanned." McCullers in the cycle explores the same apparently irresoluble conflict in Christian theology that had inspired Milton to compose *Paradise Lost:* "Why would an omnipotent God create mortals who are prone to sin?" A few of the lines, particularly in the "Incantation to

Lucifer," possess some hint of the spiritual and aesthetic strength that Milton exhibited in *Paradise Lost* and reveal her command both of rhythm and imagery:

> Angel disarmed, lay down your cunning, finally tell
> The currents, stops and altitudes between Heaven and Hell.
> Or were the scalding stars too loud for your celestial velleities,
> The everlasting zones of emptiness uncanny to your imperious hand?

She fails to sustain the heightened imaginative thrust that would have given the cycle of poems a consistent epical quality, not because of any lack of control of prosody or skill in versification, but because she attempts to use the same technique of alternating the formal with the colloquial in diction and phrasing, which she had so successfully mastered in a different medium, the short narrative. The heightened philosophical poem demands more unity and consistency than her kind of fiction did, so that the shifts from the philosophical to the mundane, from the tragic to the comic, seem incongruous in her poems, whereas in her prose, the yoking of such discordant elements often resulted in variety and a poignant irony. In the poetry the shifts appear as a lapse into the prosaic and destroy the unity of the poem, rather than creating an ironic effect. For example, in the opening poem of the long cycle she moves abruptly, after a few lines of formal incantation with lofty reference to "celestial velleities" or the angel's "imperious hand," to metaphors related to the commonplace in popular culture: "vulgar as a marathon dance," "neon lights," and "top-secret density." The alternation of colloquialisms with diction consistent with epic power is deliberate, not accidental, but her intent miscarries in the poems. McCullers attains no valid fusion of the two modes of discourse that would betoken a viable aesthetic or philosophical unity.

Nevertheless, she is responsive to the worldly and the demonic, as well as to the godly, and apparently regards knowledge of the satanic as one means of achieving spiritual wisdom. Accordingly, she prefers Lucifer to Gabriel and calls upon him to relay to her the truth about his loss of paradise and its implications for mankind. Lucifer, however, gets no chance to speak; rather, the poet continues in a monologue in the "Incantation to Lucifer," to question, to speculate, and to fantasize about his fall from grace. In "Hymen, O Hymen," her personal myth of the creation of man centers on the marriage night of God and Lucifer, in which mankind was conceived. Belief in such a means for mankind's creation signifies that mankind need encounter no fall from purity and God's grace, since the human being has had from the beginning the capacity for evil as well as for good, for sin as well as for virtue, for the godlike and for the satanic. How and why God chose Lucifer that "cosmic night" remains a mystery that McCullers never quite fully elucidates. Perhaps God in furthering the reaches of cosmic love may have deliberately chosen as mate the individual furthest from the celestial beauty and virtue that He himself represents. For mortals, the hymeneal celebration in realms beyond the stars, and its reverberating consequences, can only be symbolized by "the protean firelight fanciful in the wall," an emblumain in itself of God's spiritual power, as a love that overcomes all resistance including the demonic:

> There was no witness of this bridal night
> Only a zoic seascape and interlocking angels' might.
> So now we speculate with filial wonder,
> Fabricate that night of love and ponder
> On the quietude of Satan in our Father's arms:
> Velocity stilled, the restful shade.
> Satan we can understand—but what was God's will
> That cosmic night before we were made?

Satan becomes the protagonist and an individual of heroic stature in the first three poems of the cycle. He strides from the rim of the ocean, across the shore, with "radiant grace and arrogance." As he moves with amazing velocity into the orbit of the earth, his "visage black with wind and sun," he feels the mysterious seas begin to move awesomely with the first life, as a result of the embraces that he experienced with God.

The audaciousness characterizing "Hymen, O Hymen." McCullers also sustains in the beginning of "Love and the Rind of Time." She rephrases, "What is man that Thou art mindful of him?" with an almost sacrilegious challenge implying that, after all, man is as important as God and that the rest of creation exists for him. She asks, "What is Time that man should be so mindful?" and proceeds to move, somewhat facetiously, through several lines in which she expresses diffidence about eons, ages, centuries, or millions and billions of years —all expressed in figures ordinarily expected to impress the human mind and possibly to strike fear and awe in the heart, but for her, figures impossible to conceptualize and, therefore, meaningless. Nevertheless, she suddenly declares, in one of the abrupt transitions characteristic of her poetry, the psalmist's own sense of the overwhelming insignificance of the mortal being in the presence of God and His creation. She suggests that she even feels a kind of terror at the realization that the life of all mankind on earth has been a mere "flicker of eternity," that under the aspect of eternity the human race may be of no greater significance than the primal cell, the "essential yeast":

> What is Time that man should be so mindful:
> The earth is aged 500 thousand millions of years,

> Allowing some hundred thousand millions of margin for error
> And man evolving a mere half-million years of consciousness,
>   twilight, and terror
> Only a flicker of eternity divides us from unknowing beast
> And how far are we from the fern, the rose, essential yeast?

If McCullers in this cycle of poems considers such vast questions as the myths of creation, the battles waged on universal scale between mighty opposing forces, the millions of years of human history, and the moral complexities involved in the opposition between free choice and fate, she finally views in this third poem, "Love and the Rind of Time," such cosmic issues in light of the question that preoccupies her in many of her works of fiction—the beauty of love, the individual's need for it, his difficulty in attaining it, its inevitable fragility, and its awesome strength. McCullers hopes that a spiritual evolution, parallel to that in nature over billions of years, will allow mankind in future eons to understand the workings of love as the elemental resource that will inaugurate a true millennium at last:

> From weed to dinosaur through the peripheries of stars
> From furtherest star imperiled on the rind of time,
> How long to the core of love in human mind?

The metaphors in the fourth poem, "The Dual Angel," relate to contemporary military strategy rather than to warfare waged in distant realms many light-years ago. They center on nuclear holocaust and the possibility that other "heirs of Lucifer," like herself, may end the world and bring extinction to the human race. One recognizes that this work was composed shortly after the bombing of Hiroshima and Nagasaki. The possible imminence of atomic warfare looms large in it, and the descriptions of Nagasaki and Hiroshima project her horror at the destruction wrought by mankind: "The screams are heard by blasted ears within the radiation zone / And hanging eyes upon a cheek must see the charred and irridescent craze." The catastrophic agony that she experiences in the ruins resulting from the war cause her to cry, "Almighty God!"— an ironic exclamation, certainly, if God is omnipotent and capable of averting such tragedy. She identifies with the dazed multitudes who had no inkling that nuclear weaponry was being developed and who find themselves celebrating a joyful victory, though they are aware—but only partly—that suffering and destruction constituted that victory.

McCullers sees this century as the one interval separated from all the rest of human history and destined to become the "century of decision." She closes with a tentative optimism. Man who is capable of "transfigured vision" may yet save

the human race from "obscenest suicide," but only if he can find some way of
preventing the wholesale death and destruction that he has recently experienced.
Mankind can no longer be complacent and adopt a spectator's stance toward
what has happened, he must, rather, commit himself to some active program
of social amelioration. Human beings can no longer be like "country children
spangle-eyed at county fairs," who in their naiveté enjoy the thrill of a trapeze
performance without regard to the dangers that the acrobats daily experience.
Man's "furious intellect," McCullers in this poem views as a destructive force,
because it has, in developing the atomic bomb, exalted abstractions at the expense
of kinship among human beings. Abstract intellectualism or rationalism is satanic, not only because of the devastation of the bombed cities but also because
it can "split man from man" as it has split the atom. A Christ-like spirit of love
and a courage to search for the elusive radiance in the cold lead and steel of
modern life are the qualities that can mitigate mankind's situation if he will but
be responsive to them.

In the prayer which comprises the final poem in the cycle, "Father, Upon
Thy Image We Are Spanned," McCullers again considers the wretched aspect of
the mortal existence in face of such an evil as nuclear warfare and mankind's
possible options. She ends with the same muted hope as in the preceding poem;
but it is a tentative hope indeed, considering the evils of which human beings are
capable, the demonic propensities of the human psyche, and the thin line which
separates evil from good. Despite the horrors endemic in atomic warfare, the
individual's heart can still "blaze with Christ's vision." The almost irresoluble
problem is to inform political activity with the spirituality of which mankind is
at least intermittently capable. Good does not lie in the absence of evil, but in
the "synthesis" of good and evil which only can be wrought by God.

Though "The Twisted Trinity," "Stone Is Not Stone," and "The Dual
Angel: A Meditation on Origin and Choice" represent a considerable poetic
achievement, most significant of McCullers's poems in its craftsmanship may be
"The Mortgaged Heart." The single theme developed in it is the "mortgage"
which the beloved still holds, even after death, upon the heart of the lover, and
the positive effect upon the mourner of this continued and demanding presence
of the dead lover. Because the mourner remains inspired by his closeness to the
dead, he finds a sense of direction, a pattern for renewed living, a sharpened
sensitivity to the beauty of the world about him, and an increased sense of obli-
gation to work to satisfy its needs. Thus, in any genuine sense, mourning is not a
negative state but leads toward life instead of away from it and, in fact, doubles
one's sense of being fully alive. The survivor's joy in the apprehension of the
beauty of the world is increased, because he sees it not only with his own eyes,
but refracted also through the eyes of the dead person whom he had cherished.

Therefore, he watches twice "the orchard blossoms in gray rain" and "the cold rose skies," and gains a deepened sense of their beauty and spiritual significance. He also finds that his sense of duty is intensified since he must now react doubly to all calls made upon him. Whether the dead know of the payment of this tribute, does not really matter. Joy and virtue accrue in the life of the survivor.

The poem is characterized by great precision and compression and sustains a single thought with tautness from line to line. The simple form parallels the development of the thought. The initial three lines acknowledge the power of the dead to exact payment of love from those who mourn. The final three lines, in an ironic balance, suggest that the dead person who holds the mortgage, who seemed so imperious and demanding in the initial lines, may actually know nothing of the debt and of its conscientious repayment. That powerful one may now be simply "the secluded ash, the humble bone" and no longer involved with personal relationships.

Within this frame of opening and closing triplets, McCullers in the central eight lines develops the mourner's experience of grief and his feeling of intensified closeness to the dead. The last line, "Do the dead know?" seems, at first, not to be part of a closely unified poem. For one thing, it breaks the metrical pattern both because it is only a half-line and because it is a question. The question of whether the dead individual is sentient, however, is irrelevant in a poem which focuses upon the mourner's psyche and his salvation by means of his thoughts of the absent beloved. After McCullers's own death, her sister, Margarita Smith, edited her uncollected works and fittingly chose to call her tribute to Carson *The Mortgaged Heart* when it appeared in 1971.

LOUISE WESTLING

Carson McCullers's
Amazon Nightmare

Miss Amelia Evans is a monstrous creature, really, and yet Carson McCullers lavished admiring care in picturing her many talents, her forbidding strength, and her control of the squalid village world of *The Ballad of the Sad Café* (1943). Despite a good bit of critical attention to the novella and recent feminist interest in androgynous characters in literature, Miss Amelia's freakishness has not been seriously examined. It is crucial to the meaning of this grotesque fable, relating it closely to *The Heart Is a Lonely Hunter* and *The Member of the Wedding*. McCullers said that "Love, and especially love of a person who is incapable of returning or receiving it, is at the heart of my selection of grotesque figures to write about—people whose physical incapacity is a symbol of their spiritual incapacity to love or receive love—their spiritual isolation." But Miss Amelia's peculiarities are more specific than mere "spiritual incapacity"; they reflect McCullers's ambivalence about female identity. Miss Amelia is a grown-up tomboy whose physical proportions symbolize her exaggerated masculine self-image.

Louis Rubin is perceptive in suggesting that McCullers destroys Mick Kelley and Frankie Addams as characters when she tries to force them beyond the pain of adolescent sexual awakening into an acceptance of womanhood. She cannot really imagine such acceptance because she never found it herself. Friends often commented on her childlike manner, and her adult photos present images of the same kind of fierce boyishness she described in both Mick and Frankie. Virginia

From *Modern Fiction Studies* 28, no. 3 (Autumn 1982). © 1982 by Purdue Research Foundation.

Spencer Carr's biography amply documents the sexual ambivalence revealed most explicitly in McCullers's declaration to Nelson Algren, "I was born a man." It is this identification with the masculine that stimulates her imagination to explore the dangerous psychological territory of *The Ballad of the Sad Café*.

One critic calls McCullers's flat, childlike narrative tone "a kind of buffer to fend off what would otherwise be unbearable," but I would instead describe it as a strategy for placing the action at a safe enough remove from ordinary life to allow forbidden impulses free scope—at least for awhile. The form of *The Ballad of the Sad Café* allows McCullers to indulge the impulse to appropriate male power and thus escape the culturally inferior role of woman. There can be no other explanation for Miss Amelia's strapping physique, her skill at masculine trades, or her rejection of everything female, most apparent in her indignant refusal to play the physical part of a woman in her ten-day marriage to Marvin Macy. Her later relationship with Cousin Lymon is never threatening because he is not a real man who sees her as female. Behind the dream of independence represented by Miss Amelia's "masculinity," however, lies the fear of male vengeance which triumphs in the story's conclusion, as Marvin Macy and Cousin Lymon join forces to destroy the usurper. The formerly invincible amazon is left shrunken and imprisoned in the slowly collapsing shell of her once prosperous café.

The folktale atmosphere of *The Ballad of the Sad Café* may owe something to Isak Dinesen's *Seven Gothic Tales* (1934), whose strange ambience Carson McCullers never ceased to praise after a first reading in 1938. Dinesen's work remained very close to her, and it is quite understandable that three years later, while she struggled to resolve Frankie Addams's anxiety about growing too tall, she might have remembered Dinesen's portrait of six-foot Athena Hopballehus in "The Monkey." Probably this process was not conscious; her imagination simply revived the motif of the amazon in order to explore for herself some of the problems of sexual identity and female independence which Dinesen treats in her exotic fable. Robert S. Phillips was the first to comment on the similarities between *The Ballad of the Sad Café* and "The Monkey," but I think he overstates their extent. The only clear parallels are the motifs of the amazon and her bitter hand-to-hand combat with a hated male suitor. These motifs are developed in very different ways by the two writers, and the stories move through entirely different atmospheres to almost opposite conclusions about the sources of female autonomy. Because McCullers's novella is a kind of challenge to the arguments implied by Dinesen's story, it is useful to remind ourselves of the significance of the amazon maiden in "The Monkey."

The fairy-tale world of "The Monkey" is centered in the female dominion of Cloister Seven, a wealthy retreat for unmarried ladies and widows of noble birth. It is ruled by a virgin prioress with mysterious powers who resembles a sybil, the Chinese goddess Kuan-Yin, and the Wendish goddess of love. To all of the cloister's inhabitants it is "a fundamental article of faith that woman's loveliness and charm, which they themselves represented in their own sphere and according to their gifts, must constitute the highest inspiration and prize of life."

Athena Hopballehus embodies this ideal femininity in heroic form. She is a motherless only child who has been raised by her father in a nearby castle, surrounded by "an atmosphere of incense burnt to woman's loveliness." The father admits, however, that "she has been to me *both* son and daughter, and I have in my mind seen her wearing the old coats of armor of Hopballehus" (my italics) The problem implied in this reference to androgynous childhood training is never explored in the story, but perhaps it is meant to suggest an excess of independence. At eighteen, Athena is six feet tall, powerful and broad-shouldered, with flaming red hair and the eyes of a young lioness or eagle. Athena is what her name suggests, a human type of the warrior goddess, whom Dinesen also associates with the virgin huntress Diana and "a giant's daughter who unwittingly breaks men when she plays with them." When a proposal of marriage is made by a handsome young cavalry officer named Boris, the prioress's nephew and Athena's childhood playmate, Athena's fierce autonomy sparks an indignant refusal.

Although forceful womanhood dominates the world of "The Monkey," the story's central problem is not Athena's fate but rather the decadent weakness of the prioress's nephew Boris. This overcultivated young man is the central consciousness of the narrative, and the plot follows his reluctant entrance into normal manhood through the manipulations of his aunt. The old ladies of Cloister Seven, having heard rumors of Boris's implication in a homosexual scandal, give him an ambiguous welcome when he arrives from the capital city. They think of him as "a young priest of black magic, still within hope of conversion." A sort of conversion is indeed accomplished by the end of the story, but only because the prioress uses deception and magic to force the resisting bride and groom together. Threatening Boris by revealing her knowledge of the scandal, she induces him to drink a love potion and to force himself upon Athena. The maiden responds with her fist and knocks out two of his teeth. Dinesen tells us that all the young women Boris had previously rejected "would have felt the pride of their sex satisfied in the contemplation of his mortal pursuit of this maiden who now strove less to escape than to kill him." A fierce battle ensues, and she is about to dispatch him with a death grip on his throat when he transforms the nature of the conflict by forcing his mouth against hers. Instantly her whole body registers the terrible effect of his kiss. "As if he had run a rapier straight through her, the blood sank from her face, her body stiffened in his arms," her strength dissolved away, and she collapsed. Both Boris's and Athena's faces express "a deadly disgust" with the kiss.

In her ability to overcome even this revulsion, the prioress emerges as the very incarnation of the Wendish goddess of love, half-monkey and half-human. Because Boris and Athena witness the prioress's grotesque exchange of shapes with her monkey on the morning after the seduction attempt, they are united as initiates to the mystery of her power. They submit to her insistence that the sexes cannot remain separate; Boris must pay homage to female power, and the proud young Athena must renounce her heroic virginity in an alliance with him.

No union of male and female, however reluctant, occurs in *The Ballad of the Sad Café*. In contrast to Athena's essentially female power, Miss Amelia's remarkable strength depends on her masculinity in a world devoid of feminine qualities. All the characters who have speaking parts are males, except for Miss Amelia, who never betrays even a hint of conventionally feminine behavior.

Like Dinesen's Athena, Miss Amelia is a motherless only child raised by an adoring father, but McCullers gives her amazon a more exaggerated physique and a mysterious authority. At the height of her adult pride, Miss Amelia is the central personality of her town. An imposing figure, she is "a dark, tall woman with bones and muscles like a man," hairy thighs, and short-cropped hair brushed back from her forehead like Mick Kelley's and Frankie Addams's. In the building she inherited from her father, she operates a profitable general store which gradually becomes the town's only café. She produces the best liquor in the county from her secret still in a nearby swamp; sells chitterlins, sausage, and golden sorghum molasses; owns farms in the vicinity; and is adept at all manual skills, such as carpentry, masonry, and butchery. The most impressive of all her powers, however, and the one that with the magical properties of her whiskey best reveals her nearly supernatural dimensions, is her ability to heal the sick. Like a sorceress or witch, she brews her own secret remedies from roots and herbs. "In the face of the most dangerous and extraordinary treatment she did not hesitate, and no disease was so terrible but what she would undertake to cure it."

There is one notable exception to Miss Amelia's healing powers:

> If a patient came with a female complaint she could do nothing. Indeed at the mere mention of the words her face would slowly darken with shame, and she would stand there craning her neck against the collar of her shirt, or rubbing her swamp boots together, for all the world like a great, shamed, dumb-tongued child.

Her embarrassed confusion is a natural consequence of her total identification with masculinity and her childlike sexual innocence. Even in adulthood, Miss Amelia preserves the tomboy attitudes we encounter in Mick Kelley and Frankie Addams. For all of these characters, the first physical encounters with men are unpleasant surprises. We remember Mick's distaste for her one experience of lovemaking with Harry Minowitz and Frankie's terrified escape from the soldier who tried to seduce her. For both Mick and Frankie, sexual experience brought the necessary renunciation of childhood boyish freedom and a reluctant acceptance of adult femininity. But Miss Amelia refuses to accept the diminished status of woman. When she rather absentmindedly marries Marvin Macy, the whole town is relieved, expecting marriage to soften her character and physique "and to change her at last into a calculable woman." Instead, after the bridegroom follows her upstairs to bed on their wedding night, Miss Amelia stamps downstairs in a rage, wearing breeches and a khaki jacket. Until dawn she reads the Farmer's Almanac, smokes her father's pipe, and practices on her new typewriter. During the ensuing ten days of the abortive marriage, she sleeps downstairs and continues to ignore her husband unless he comes within striking range, when she socks him with her fist. Macy disappears from town in disgrace, leaving Amelia victorious in her amazon virginity.

For ten uneventful years Miss Amelia goes about her solitary life, aloof, stingy, maintaining her strange control of the town. Then one night the little hunchbacked Cousin Lymon mysteriously appears on her doorstep, wins her heart, and causes momentous changes both in her life and in the life of the town for six years before the sinister return of Marvin Macy. The question is why Miss Amelia should have rejected a vigorous normal man, only to fall in love with a twisted midget. Joseph Millichap sees traditional folktale elements in the characters of Marvin Macy and Cousin Lymon: Macy is a sort of demon lover, and Cousin Lymon is reminiscent of the figures of mysterious stranger and elf. But Millichap comes closer to answering our question when he says that Cousin Lymon "is a man loved without sex, a child acquired without pain, and a companion which her [Amelia's] limited personality finds more acceptable than a husband or a child." Marvin Macy had been sufficiently ennobled by his love for Miss Amelia so that he might have been a tolerable mate for her, but, by accepting her feminine part in the marriage, Amelia would have had to renounce the masculine sources of her strength. Such a capitulation to the female mysteries that she has avoided all her life would be unthinkable. Her enraged reaction to Macy's forlorn attempts at lovemaking clearly expresses the insult they represent to her pride. Cousin Lymon, on the other hand, represents no threat to her power. He is a sickly, deformed mannikin whom she could crush with one blow of her fist, and, from all we can see, he makes no sexual demands. His warped, childlike form clearly indicates his masculine impotence, just as Amelia's grotesquely masculine appearance expresses her inability to function as a woman. With Lymon she feels safe in revealing affection, for she can baby and pet him without any threat of sexuality.

At the heart of Miss Amelia's relationship with Cousin Lymon, there is actually an inversion of traditional roles of male and female. Miss Amelia is physically dominant and provides a living for the household as a husband would. Cousin Lymon is the pampered mate who struts about in finery, is finicky about food and accommodations, and gads about town socializing and gossiping. He functions as a hostess would in the café, while Miss Amelia stands aloof and silent in the background. In their intimate conversations before the parlor fire, Miss Amelia sits with her "long legs stretched out before the hearth" contemplating philosophical problems and reminiscing about her father, while Cousin Lymon sits wrapped in a blanket or green shawl on a low chair and chatters endlessly about petty details.

Despite his physical weakness and his vanity, Cousin Lymon seems to embody the spirit of spring and renewal. He has drifted mysteriously into town in April, in a year when the crops promise well and conditions at the local mill are relatively prosperous. Once accepted as Miss Amelia's intimate, he becomes a catalyst for the release of her genial impulses. Her devotion to him brightens her face and gradually engenders a hospitality she had never expressed before. Before the hunchback's arrival, she sold her moonshine by the bottle, handing it out through her back door in the dark. Never was anyone allowed to open or to drink this liquor inside the building. But once Cousin Lymon is installed in her house, she begins selling it inside, providing glasses and plates of crackers for consumption on the premises. Gradually the store is transformed into a café with tables where Miss Amelia sells liquor by the drink and serves fried catfish suppers for fifteen cents a plate. Miss Amelia grows more sociable and less inclined to cheat her business associates. Even her special powers for healing and for brewing her marvelous liquor are enhanced. All these positive developments of her character expand themselves in the communal warmth which her café comes to provide for the town.

Though Cousin Lymon brings fruitful changes in the lives of Miss Amelia and her town, his own physical state suggests a fatal limitation to prosperity. He remains "weakly and deformed" despite Amelia's pampering and the exercise of her fullest healing abilities. He is also personally malicious, even though he has generally served as an agent for gaiety and warmth. Thus he is naturally drawn to the cruel strength of Marvin Macy, a force which complements his own unpleasant traits. When Macy suddenly returns to town from years in the state penitentiary, Cousin Lymon is immediately infatuated.

Macy embodies all the qualities of "normal" masculinity, but McCullers has cast them in an evil, destructive light throughout the story. Macy may be tall, brawny, and good-looking, but he is also violent and viciously lustful. He is the devil male who mutilates animals for fun and has ruined the tenderest young girls in the region. Amelia refers to Macy's cloven hoof, and the satanic is also suggested by his red shirt and the fact that he never sweats. Throughout the story he is allied with winter. Even though he had been temporarily reformed by his love for Miss Amelia, their wedding took place on a winter day rather than in the traditionally propitious season of spring or of summer. His revengeful return to town sixteen years later comes in autumn and brings sinister portents of unseasonable weather, ruining the normally festive ritual of hog butchering: "there was everywhere the smell of slowly spoiling meat, and an atmosphere of dreary waste." Macy lays claim to the unprecedented snowfall in January that gives the town "a drawn, bleak look." The climactic battle between Miss Amelia and Marvin Macy occurs exactly one month later, on Groundhog Day. Its issue is foreordained by Cousin Lymon's report that the groundhog has seen its shadow and, therefore, that more winter lies ahead.

Understanding at once that Macy's return to town is a challenge, Miss Amelia begins preparations for a fight, taunting Macy by wearing her red dress as a flagrant reminder of his failure to make her act the part of a woman during their marriage. While she wears the dress, she pokes her biceps constantly, practices lifting heavy objects, and works out with a punching bag in her yard. In the climactic battle between the two antagonists, the question to be decided is not, as in Dinesen, whether a powerful young woman can be subdued so that a union of the sexes can occur. For McCullers, the contest will decide whether a woman can deny her sex and dominate men with a strength analogous to their own.

> Now the test had come, and in these moments of terrible effort, it was Miss Amelia who was the stronger. Marvin Macy was greased and slippery, tricky to grasp, but she was stronger. Gradually she bent him over backward, and inch by inch she forced him to the floor. . . . At last she had him down, and straddled; her strong big hands were on his throat.

Suddenly, at this moment of Miss Amelia's triumph, Cousin Lymon leaps across the room from his perch on the bar to aid his adored male friend. He lands on Amelia's back and changes the balance of force to Macy's advantage. Miss Amelia is destroyed.

The sexual dynamics of *The Ballad of the Sad Café* are an inversion of traditional heterosexual patterns. Contrasts with Dinesen's "The Monkey" help reveal the masculine sources of Miss Amelia's autonomous strength and point up McCullers's complete rejection of heterosexual union. Rather than accepting her femininity by consummating her marriage to the aggressively masculine Marvin Macy, Miss Amelia focuses her affections on the little hunchback who seems to function simultaneously as child, pet, and rather feminine companion. But Cousin Lymon is much less devoted to Miss Amelia than she is to him, and this gives him an emotional advantage over her which proves ultimately disastrous. It seems inevitable that the foppish dwarf should fall helplessly in love with Marvin Macy, thus completing the destructive triangular relationship which McCullers used to develop her theory that "almost everyone wants to be the lover" and that "in a deep secret way, the state of being loved is intolerable to many." But this theory and McCullers's statement that *Ballad* was intended to show the inferiority of passionate individual love to *agape* fail to account for the individual peculiarities of her characters and for the sexual dimensions of their problems in love. The real force of *The Ballad of the Sad Café* lies in its depiction of a masculine amazon whose transgression of conventional sexual boundaries brings catastrophic male retribution. Unlike Dinesen, who portrayed an uneasy compromise between proud female autonomy and reluctant masculine homage, McCullers sought to deny the feminine entirely and to allow a woman to function successfully as a man. She could not sustain her vision because she knew it was impossible. I believe that the consequences of her experiment in this novella play a part in determining the final form of *The Member of the Wedding*, which, as I have argued elsewhere, inexorably moves Frankie toward an acceptance of conventional femininity. After writing *The Ballad of the Sad Café* in only a few months, when McCullers returned to her six-year struggle with the materials of *The Member of the Wedding*, she knew that Frankie would have to submit as Miss Amelia had not.

MARY ANN DAZEY

Two Voices of the Single Narrator
in The Ballad of the Sad Café

When *The Ballad of the Sad Café* was first published in *Harper's Bazaar* in 1943, Carson McCullers was twenty-six, and at that time most critics pointed to the work as evidence of the great promise of the young writer. Today, however, it is ranked along with *The Member of the Wedding* as her most successful work. McCullers's choosing to call the sad, romantic tale a ballad has caused many to discuss her ballad style in some fashion. In his work *Carson McCullers*, Lawrence Graver, for example, concludes that *The Ballad of the Sad Café* is one of her most "rewarding works" in part because she employed "a relaxed colloquial style, punctuating the narrative with phrases like 'time must pass' and 'so do not forget.'" Ironically, Dayton Kohler, eighteen years earlier, had selected these identical lines as evidence of McCullers's "stylistic coyness," which he called "poetically false and out of the context with the objective drama." He further determined that the passages where the narrator stops the flow of the story to make "wise observations" indicate McCullers's own feelings that her story was "too weak to carry unsupported its burden of theme and sensibility." Both critics are reacting to what Dawson F. Gaillard determines is the changing voice of the narrator. Gaillard points out that in the first paragraph of the story, for example, the narrator's voice is "flat" and "inflectionless" and Is "adjusted" to the "dreariness" of the town; then it changes and loses the flatness to become the ballad teller. This ballad maker, Joseph R. Millichap concludes, "fixes the style of the novel." His voice permits McCullers to weave her literary ballad into a perfect blend of the "literate and colloquial."

From *The Southern Literary Journal* 17, no. 2 (Spring 1985). © 1985 by the Department of English of the University of North Carolina at Chapel Hill.

A stylistic analysis of *The Ballad of the Sad Café* reveals that McCullers has created a single narrator with two distinctly different voices. In the first voice the narrator places the characters and their actions in the mainstream of human existence. This voice begins, "The town itself is dreary" and ends, "Yes, the town is dreary." This voice concludes the introduction, "You might as well walk down to the Forks Falls Road and listen to the chain gang" and ends the story, "You might as well go down to the Forks Falls highway and listen to the chain gang." Not only does this voice provide the frame for the drama, but it also flows throughout the story as a second voice of the single narrator. In this voice the reader is sometimes addressed directly and even commanded to respond to the narration.

For the voice of the ballad maker, who actually tells the tale of Miss Amelia, her ten-day bridegroom, and her cousin Lymon, McCullers chooses past-tense verb forms. When the first voice, the voice of the lamenter, encountered at the beginning of the novel, speaks, McCullers chooses present-tense verb forms. The first shift occurs after Cousin Lymon has appeared and has been offered a drink of Miss Amelia's whiskey. The narrator explains:

> The whiskey they drank that evening (two big bottles of it) is important. Otherwise, it would be hard to account for what followed. Perhaps without it there would never have been a café. For the liquor of Miss Amelia has a special quality of its own. It is clean and sharp on the tongue, but once down a man it glows inside him for a long time afterward. And that is not all. It is known that if a message is written with lemon juice on a clean sheet of paper there will be no sign of it. But if the paper is held for a moment to the fire then the letters turn brown and the meaning becomes clear.

Next this voice draws the reader into the experience, and McCullers employs the first of eight imperatives that run throughout the first half of the novel (italics in quotations mine):

> *Imagine* that the whiskey is the fire and that the message is that which is known only in the soul of a man—then the worth of Miss Amelia's liquor can be understood. Things that have gone unnoticed, thoughts that have been harbored far back in the dark mind are suddenly recognized and comprehended.

The second of the eight imperatives occurs after the regular group of townsmen has been named and described. The ballad maker says, "Each of them worked in the mill, and lived with others in a two- or three-room house for which the rent was ten dollars or twelve dollars a month. All had been paid that afternoon, for it was Saturday." And the lamenting voice adds, "So, for the present, *think* of them as a whole."

In the third imperative, the narrator becomes a camera which provides a long shot of Miss Amelia and Cousin Lymon as the two establish a pattern of behavior over the years:

> So for the moment *regard* these years from random and disjointed views. *See* the hunchback marching in Miss Amelia's footsteps when on a red winter morning they set out for the pinewoods to hunt. *See* them working on her properties — with Cousin Lymon standing by and doing absolutely nothing, but quick to point out any laziness among the hands. On autumn afternoons they sat on the back steps chopping sugar cane. The glaring summer days they spent back in the swamp where the water cypress is a deep black green, where beneath the tangled swamp trees there is a drowsy gloom. When the path leads through a bog or a stretch of blackened water *see* Miss Amelia bend down to let Cousin Lymon scramble on her back — and *see* her wading forward with the hunchback settled on her shoulders, clinging to her ears or to her broad forehead.
>
> For the hunchback was sickly at night and dreaded to lie looking into the dark. He had a deep fear of death. And Miss Amelia would not leave him by himself to suffer with this fright. It may even be reasoned that the growth of the café came about mainly on this account; it was a thing that brought him through the night. So *compose* from such flashes an image of these years as a whole. And for a moment *let* it rest.

The next imperative instructs the reader in his understanding of Miss Amelia's peculiar behavior and prepares him for the story of Marvin Macy and Miss Amelia's ten-day marriage: "*Remember* that it all happened long ago, and that it was Miss Amelia's only personal contact, before the hunchback came to her, with this phenomenon — love." And at the end of the recital of events concerning the brief marriage and Marvin Macy's departure from town, this voice again addresses the reader, "So *do* not *forget* this Marvin Macy, as he is to act a terrible part in the story which is yet to come." The final instructions to the reader are delivered when Marvin Macy is about to return to town and change the lives of Miss Amelia and Cousin Lymon forever: "So *let* the slow years pass and come to a Saturday evening six years after the time when Cousin Lymon came first to the town."

Constantly flowing alongside these imperatives and the lively voice of the

ballad maker are the generalizations made by the lamenting voice about the specific actions of the characters. The specific action of a character is told in past
tense, but the interpretation is always in the present tense. Of Cousin Lymon,
the subjective narrator explains, "There is a type of person who *has* a quality
about him that sets him apart from other and more ordinary human beings.
Such a person *has* an instinct to establish immediate and vital contact between
himself and all things in the world." And the ballad maker observes, "Certainly
the hunchback *was* of this type." And after the ballad maker tells the story of the
miserable lives of the Macy children, the lamenting voice explains what this background does to Henry Macy:

> But the hearts of small children *are* delicate organs. A cruel beginning
> in this world *can twist* them into curious shapes. The heart of a hurt
> child *can shrink* so that forever afterward it is hard and pitted as the
> seed of a peach. Or again, the heart of such a child *may fester* and
> *swell* until it is a misery to carry within the body, easily chafed and
> hurt by the most ordinary things. This last *is* what happened to
> Henry Macy, who *is* so opposite to his brother, *is* the kindest and
> gentlest man in town.

Of the two voices of the narrator, the one which tells the love story, the
actual narrative, is the dominant one. This voice is the objective voice of the
literary ballad maker. On this level, McCullers chooses past-tense verb forms,
simple diction, a large percentage of simple sentences, often as short as three or
four words, compound sentences with short members, and realistic dialog. The
dialog is in rural Georgia dialect and comprises a very small percentage of the
total narrative, actually less than one hundred and fifty lines. Like Eudora Welty,
McCullers relies entirely on syntax and local idiom to convey the speech patterns
of these rural mill-town people. She does not employ distortion of spelling to
convey variances in pronunciation. Although the narrator implies that long hours
of the long, hot summers and dreary winters were spent in telling tall tales, little
actual evidence of any prolonged conversation exists in the novel. Only once is
there a sustained conversation between Miss Amelia and Cousin Lymon:

> "Amelia, what does it signify?" Cousin Lymon asked her. "Why, it's
> just an acorn," she answered. "Just an acorn I picked up on the after-
> noon Big Papa died."
> "How do you mean?" Cousin Lymon insisted.
> "I mean it's just an acorn I spied on the ground that day. I picked
> it up and put it in my pocket. But I don't know why."
> "What a peculiar reason to keep it," Cousin Lymon said.

In an apparent imitation of the poetic ballad, McCullers constructs paragraphs which are rather uniform in length, about one hundred and fifty words each. Many of these paragraphs begin with very short simple sentences in subject verb order:

The place was not always a cage.

Dark came on.

And Miss Amelia married him.

They were wrong.

The hunchback chattered on.

Henry Macy was still silent.

The hunchback was impatient.

The autumn was a happy time.

No one answered.

Miss Amelia made no protest.

The snow did not last.

So things went on like this.

The rest is confusion.

Additionally in the literary ballad form McCullers employs alliteration, repetition, and poetic imagery. Running throughout the narrative are repeated references to Miss Amelia's "ten-day marriage," "the loom-fixer," "the August white heat," "the peach trees," "the golden dust." She paints her background canvas with color imagery:

The *red* winter sun was setting, and to the west the sky was deep *gold* and *crimson*.

The next morning was serene, with a sunrise of warm *purple* mixed with *rose*. In the fields around the town the furrows were newly plowed, and very early the tenants were at work setting out the young, deep *green* tobacco plants. The wild crows flew down close to the fields, making swift *blue* shadows on the earth. In the town the people set out early with their dinner pails, and the windows of the mill were blinding *gold* in the sun.

McCullers most frequently employs alliteration and sensory images, often combining the two:

> The moon made dim, twisted shadows of the blossoming peach trees along the side of the road. In the air the odor of blossoms and sweet spring grass mingled with the warm, sour smell of the near-by lagoon.

> The night was silent and the moon still shone with a soft, clear light —it was getting colder.

> The lamp on the table was well-trimmed, burning blue at the edges of the wick and casting a cheerful light in the kitchen.

The two voices of the single narrator alternate and together weave the tale of the lover, the beloved and of love betrayed. The ballad voice tells the story, and the second voice provides the sad background music. The styles of the two voices are distinctly different in syntax also. In the ballad teller's voice, McCullers rarely employs complex sentences. When they are used, they are almost always in normal order with single right-branching clauses. The most common of these structures is the noun modifier rather than an adverbial modifier. Unlike the simple sentences which often have tricolon verb structures with the last member expanded, the complex sentences usually employ either a single verb or a compound verb. On the other hand, the lamenting voice is related in complex sentences in periodic order with multiple clauses that are both adverbial and adjectival. These structures often employ self-embeddings along with multiple nominals and verbals.

This analysis would seem to imply that one voice is entirely separate from the other; that, however, is not the case. The transitions from one voice to the other are smooth, almost unnoticeable. One of the transitional devices that McCullers employs to move from one to the other is the question and answer. The ballad teller asks a question, and the lamenting voice answers it:

> What sort of thing, then was this love?
>
> First of all, love is a joint experience between two persons—but the fact that it is a joint experience to the two people involved. There are the lover and the beloved, but these two come from different countries. Often the beloved is only a stimulus for all the stored-up love which has lain quiet within the lover for a long time hitherto. And somehow every lover knows this. He feels in his soul that his love is a solitary thing. He comes to know a new, strange loneliness

and it is this knowledge which makes him suffer. So there is only one thing for the lover to do. He must house his lover within himself as best he can; he must create for himself a whole new inward world —a world intense and strange, complete in himself.

The most frequently used device is the shift from the particular action of the mill-town group to the lamenting voice's generalization about that pattern of behavior among all people, as when McCullers moves from a description of Henry Macy as a child to her generalization about all such miserable children, or from Miss Amelia's liquor to the effects of liquor in general. This particular technique also permits transition again to the narrative in the reverse pattern of general to particular. For example, after the ballad teller has described the birth of the café, the lamenting voice comments on the general behavior of people in cafés, and the ballad teller follows this philosophical comment with the behavior of Miss Amelia's customers:

> But the spirit of a café is altogether different. Even the richest, greediest old rascal will behave himself, insulting no one in a proper café. And poor people look about them gratefully and pinch up the salt in a dainty and modest manner. For the atmosphere of a proper café implies these qualities: fellowship, the satisfactions of the belly, and a certain gaiety and grace of behavior. This had never been told to the gathering in Miss Amelia's store that night. But they knew it of themselves, although never, of course, until that time had there been a café in the town.

The third method of transition from one voice to the other employed by McCullers is the time shift from the past of the story to the present. Of course the novel begins and ends in the present in the "dreary" mill town, but constantly within the frame of this time, the reader is swept back from the lively past into the present. The reader is carefully reminded that "it all happened long ago."

After the narrator's two voices are silent, after the sad story has been told, McCullers attaches the epilogue "Twelve Mortal Men." Barbara Nauer Folk believes that this epilogue serves to remind the reader that the story is both a "literary ballad and a folk dirge." What Folk is isolating in form as "dual-level usage of the ballad form" is stylistically the dual voices of the single narrator. The harmony of the voices of the "twelve mortal men, seven of them black and five of them white boys from this country" is precisely the kind of harmony McCullers achieves in the blending of the two voices of her single narrator. For the objective voice that relates the sequence of events of the narrative, McCullers chooses short, almost choppy sentences in normal order and casts the verbs in the past tense. For the subjective, lamenting voice, she employs long sentences with multiple embeddings, present tense verb forms, and frequent imperatives that order the reader to interpret the bare details given by the other voice. These two voices serve McCullers in the same way that various instruments within an orchestra serve the conductor. The harmony is not achieved because the various musicians are reacting to the same notes; it relies upon the instructions of that conductor. That the two distinctly different narrative voices in *The Ballad of the Sad Café* are not in discord is a tribute to the author's ability to convey these voices in two recognizably different yet compatible rhetorical styles.

BARBARA A. WHITE

Loss of Self in The Member
of the Wedding

*"The greatest danger, that of losing one's own self, may pass off as if it
were nothing; every other loss, that of an arm, a leg, five dollars, a wife
[sic], etc., is sure to be noticed."*
> —KIERKEGAARD, quoted by J. T. Malone in
> McCullers's *Clock Without Hands*

Carson McCullers's *The Member of the Wedding* (1946) takes place in a small
southern town where the protagonist, Frankie Addams, lives with her father.
During the hot August of the novel Frankie spends her time in the Addamses'
kitchen with the black cook, Berenice, and her six-year-old cousin, John Henry.
She becomes enchanted with her brother's approaching wedding, decides to join
the wedding and the honeymoon, and is disillusioned when her plan fails.

Although Frankie is only "twelve and five-sixths years old," there is much
about her which will immediately seem familiar. She makes her appearance
dressed as a boy, though she also douses herself with Sweet Serenade perfume;
she hesitates on the threshold of the kitchen, being "an unjoined person who
hung around in doorways." In the first few pages of the novel we learn that
Frankie fears the future and resists even the knowledge of sex, which she calls
"nasty lies about married people." Her hometown might just as well be North
Dormer or Buena Vista, for Frankie wants out: "I've been ready to leave this
town so long. . . . I wish I had a hundred dollars and could just light out and
never see this town again."

From *Growing Up Female: Adolescent Girlhood in American Fiction.* © 1985 by Barbara
A. White. Greenwood Press, 1985. Originally entitled "Loss of Self in Carson McCullers' *The Member of the Wedding.*"

125

In light of Frankie's resemblance to her predecessors in the novel of adolescence, it is surprising that a well-read critic like Edmund Wilson could not determine what the novel is about. Wilson, in a review which infuriated McCullers, declared that "the whole story seems utterly pointless." McCullers had the same problem when she tried to market her dramatic version of *Member*: "Few [producers] seemed to know what the play was really about." Subsequent readers have turned to her other works in attempt to explain *Member*. Since one of McCullers's continuing themes is spiritual isolation, most critics interpret Frankie's fear of the future as the universal fear of separate identity and her attempt to join her brother's wedding as representative of all people's struggle to overcome their final separateness from other humans. Thus Frankie becomes a "symbol of spiritual loneliness."

Alternatively, Frankie is thought to symbolize the grotesqueness of the human condition. If Carson McCullers writes about isolation, she also includes in her novels a large number of "freaks": deaf-mutes, alcoholics, idiots, hunchbacked dwarves, etc. Frankie, having seen such beings as the Giant, the Pin Head, and the Alligator Boy at the fair, worries that she herself may become a freak; she calculates that if she continues growing at her present rate she will be over nine feet tall. Some readers have taken Frankie's fear literally and regarded *Member* as another examination by McCullers of the "freakish and perverse." Frankie becomes a "little monster" illustrating the general wretchedness of humanity.

Neither the "freak" nor the "spiritual isolation" approach turns out to be helpful in interpreting *The Member of the Wedding*. It is difficult to understand just what is "freakish" about Frankie; if she occasionally lies and steals and dresses up in garish costumes, so does Huckleberry Finn, nobody's idea of a freak. Frankie makes a more promising symbol of spiritual isolation, but isolation is only one theme of *Member* and does not in itself allow us to account for the rich detail of the novel. The eagerness of critics to make her symbolic suggests some anxiety over the subject of female adolescence. To some extent we can see this anxiety operating in critical reaction to Wharton's *Summer* and Suckow's fiction. *Summer* was thought to be about New England life or Lawyer Royall, anything but a girl growing up; Suckow's novels were labelled too domestic and too "intrinsically feminine." But *Summer* and Suckow could easily be ignored— *Summer* relegated to the position of a "minor" novel in Wharton's oeuvre and Suckow dismissed altogether. *The Member of the Wedding*, as the long-awaited novel of a young "genius," invited more extensive critical response. Interestingly, the major part of this response has been barely concealed disappointment at the subject of McCullers's novel, feeling that it deals with only "a narrow corner of human existence." Although, as I noted in my preface, male initiation is con-

sidered a significant subject for novelists to treat, female initiation is not perceived as equally "universal." Thus most critics have tried to make *Member* about
something other than female adolescence, such as isolation or freakdom; they
have avoided any discussion of the gender of the protagonist.

Not surprisingly, it was Leslie Fiedler who introduced the question of gender when he characterized Frankie as one of McCullers's "boy-girls," her "trans-
vestite Huckleberry Finns." Once we have seen how McCullers portrays Frankie's
adolescence, I will return to criticism of *The Member of the Wedding* and show
how Fiedler also set a precedent in sexist interpretation of McCullers's "boy-
girls," whereby her literary reputation is disparaged; for now the point is that
Frankie's gender has at least been admitted as relevant. Taking his cue from Fiedler, Chester Eisinger says:

> The adolescent girl, in Mrs. McCullers's fiction, has the problem not
> only of sex awareness but of sex determination. It is not the respon-
> sibility of womanhood that she reluctantly must take up but the
> decision to be a woman at all that she must make. She is, then sex-
> less, hovering between the two sexes.

This decision which confronts her, "the decision to be a woman at all,"
accounts in large part for Frankie's fear and forms a major thematic concern of
The Member of the Wedding. Eisinger's term "sexless" has no meaning, since
Frankie's "sex determination" was made at birth; however, she is "hovering between the two sexes" in the sense that she is a girl who does not want to relin-
quish the privileges of boys. Like Ruth Suckow's heroines, Frankie exists in a
divided state: while she hesitates to stay in childhood, she cannot fulfill her desire
to be "grown-up" without accepting her identity as female, and she already suspects that her gender will be confining. Frankie thus vacillates between striving
for adult status and resisting it.

Frankie's reluctance to remain a child is shown in her outrage at being given
a doll by her brother Jarvis and his fiancée. She also resents being addressed as a
child and peppers her own language with such grown-up phrases as "sick unto
death" and "irony of fate." The most obvious sign of Frankie's projected change
of identity from child to adult is her revision of her name from "Frankie" to
"F. Jasmine." While "Frankie" is a child's name, "F. Jasmine" sounds older.
Frankie chooses "Jasmine" partly because the initial "Ja" matches the "Ja" of
Jarvis and Janice, but "Jasmine," associated with sweet fragrance and pale yellow
flowers, has obvious, romantic, "feminine" connotations. Growing up necessitates
shedding a "masculine" name, clothing, and activities for "feminine" ones.

In many ways Frankie wants to make this change. When she becomes F.
Jasmine she vows to give up being "rough and greedy." Most important, she

attempts to change her appearance. Apart from her name, Frankie's most obvious "tomboy" badges are her crewcut and her typical costume of shorts, undervest, and cowboy hat. As F. Jasmine she wears a pink organdie dress, heavy lipstick, and Sweet Serenade perfume. She cannot alter her hair style immediately but she knows what women "should" look like; "I ought to have long bright yellow hair," Frankie thinks.

Frankie's avatar, Mick Kelly of McCullers's *The Heart Is a Lonely Hunter* (1940), undergoes the same transformation. At first Mick resists her older sisters when they try to make her stop wearing "those silly boys' clothes." In a passage reminiscent of Jo March's pulling off her hair net, she exclaims:

> "I wear shorts because I don't want to wear your old hand-me-downs. I don't want to be like either of you and I don't want to look like either of you. And I won't. That's why I wear shorts. I'd rather be a boy any day."

But eventually Mick practices dressing up in her older sisters' evening gowns. She decides she is too old to wear shorts and switches permanently to skirts.

Both Mick's and Frankie's attempts to imitate the dress of adult women are confused and naive. The pleats and hem of Mick's skirt have come out, and to other characters in the novel she still looks as much like a boy as a girl. For her brother's wedding Frankie buys a cheap orange satin evening dress and silver slippers, revealing that she does not yet understand society's division of women into "nice" (pink organdie) and "not nice" (orange satin). Furthermore, as Berenice points out, a woman's evening dress and the brown crust on Frankie's elbows do not mix. Even the new "feminine" name "F. Jasmine" is ambiguous because it is generally a male practice to use an initial and a middle name. One might conclude that Frankie is unconsciously subverting her outward attempt to become more womanly.

But even if Frankie approaches the "feminine" art of self-decoration with ambivalence, it is significant that she cares about her appearance. Frankie dislikes what she considers her "dark ugly mug"; as we noted earlier, she worries that she is too tall and will be a nine-foot freak. Her preoccupation with freaks has been linked to her fear of isolation; however, to Frankie the true horror of freakdom is the horror of being an *ugly woman*, of not being able to live up to the name "Jasmine." Frankie's questions to Berenice "Do you think I will grow into a Freak?" and "Do you think I will be pretty?" are joined together, and her association of looks and male approval becomes clear when she tells Berenice she doubts that freaks ever get married.

Since marriage has traditionally been woman's fate, it is logical that in contemplating growing up Frankie should turn to thoughts of love, sex, and marriage. The younger Frankie had scorned love and left it out of her homemade shows; preferring movies about criminals, cowboys, and war, she caused a disturbance when the local theatre showed *Camille*. But now she recalls the time when she committed a "queer sin" with the neighbor boy Barney MacKean and the time when she surprised one of the Addams's boarders in bed with his wife "having a fit." She thinks about love and becomes fascinated with her brother's wedding. If the wedding provides an opportunity for Frankie to escape her loneliness and become a "member" of something, it is also the marriage of a man and a woman, and in her obsession with a wedding, Frankie anticipates her own destiny. Instead of stopping her ears as she used to when Berenice talked of love and marriage, Frankie now encourages Berenice and listens to her carefully.

Whatever difficulties Frankie has in making the "decision to be a woman" cannot be attributed to her lack of a mother because Berenice performs a motherly function in initiating Frankie into her expected role. Berenice correctly interprets Frankie's concern with the wedding as concern with her own future as a woman. Thus Berenice suggests that Frankie acquire a "nice little white boy beau." Berenice's advice to Frankie is a classic compression of traditional "womanly wisdom." She says: "Now you belong to change from being so rough and greedy and big. You ought to fix yourself up nice in your dresses. And speak sweetly and act sly." In three sentences Berenice has summarized the major traits girls are taught to cultivate in preparation for their relationships with men: "object" orientation ("fix yourself up nice"), passivity and submission ("speak sweetly"), and calculation and trickery ("act sly"). No real mother could do a more thorough job of socialization.

Critics have been unanimous in viewing Berenice as a positive influence on Frankie. They consider her wise and spiritual, a mouthpiece for McCullers and the "Socrates of the novel." However, McCullers presents Berenice as a completely man-oriented woman. For her to talk about her life means to talk about her four previous husbands and current beau. Berenice communicates to Frankie pride in the number of men one can attract. When John Henry asks her how many beaus she "caught," she replies: "Lamb, how many hairs is in these plaits? You talking to Berenice Sadie Brown." Berenice feels proud that men "treat" her, that she doesn't have to "pay her own way." Besides, the company of men is preferable to that of women; she proclaims, "I'm not the kind of person to go around with crowds of womens."

It is surprising how much Berenice resembles a mother who has been the object of much vituperation from critics, Amanda Wingfield of Tennessee Williams's *The Glass Menagerie* (1944). In this play by McCullers's close friend, Amanda tries to transform her shy daughter into a southern belle. Berenice is in most ways a more attractive character than Amanda; yet her cataloging of her past in terms of beaus is much like Amanda's in terms of "gentlemen callers," and her advice to her reluctant young charge is exactly the same as Amanda's to her daughter.

Much of the humor in *The Member of the Wedding* involves the young and unworldly Frankie and John Henry, but we are not allowed to forget that Berenice also is limited in her perceptions. For instance, Frankie asks Berenice why she married at the youthful age of thirteen (Frankie is almost thirteen herself). Berenice responds, "Because I wanted to. I were thirteen years old and I haven't growed a inch since." Frankie, who we know worries about her height, asks, "Does marrying really stop your growth?" "It certainy do," replies Berenice, unaware of the implications of her statement. In this case, the author has distanced herself from Berenice, creating an irony involving her.

Furthermore, the Berenice who in the middle of the novel rejects Frankie's advice that she marry her latest beau, T. T. Williams, ends up by taking it. Frankie tells Berenice to "quit worrying about beaus and be content with T. T. I bet you are forty years old. It is time for you to settle down." Berenice asserts that she will not marry T. T. because he doesn't "make her shiver." She rebukes Frankie, saying, "I got many a long year ahead of me before I resign myself to a corner." But finally Berenice decides that she "might as well" marry T. T. In other words, her experience in the novel is not at a level above Frankie's but parallels it. Berenice, like Frankie, hates sleeping alone, and she submits, resigning herself to a corner, just as Frankie finally gives up her dreams and accepts the role marked out for her.

Even with Berenice's tutelage and her own desire to be treated as an adult, Frankie fears growing up. It is not simply that she might fail to meet the standards of womanhood (be the proper height, be pretty, etc.)—Frankie feels especially afraid when she "thinks about the world." She reads the war news in the paper and wants

> to be a boy and go to war as a Marine. She thought about flying aeroplanes and winning gold medals for bravery. But she could not join the war, and this made her sometimes feel restless and blue. . . .
> To think about the world for very long made her afraid. She was not afraid of Germans or bombs or Japanese. She was afraid because in the war they would not include her, and because the world seemed somehow separate from herself.

She envies the soldiers she sees in town for their mobility, the opportunity they have to travel and see the world—in other words, to gain experience. Frankie feels left out. When she wonders "who she was, and what she was going to be in the world," she gets a "queer tightness in her chest."

No doubt many a boy has had the same thirst for adventure and felt frustrated by his youth. But it is not just a question of youth for Frankie, any more than it is for Richard Wright's Bigger Thomas. When he sees a plane overhead, Bigger tells his friend Gus, "I could fly one of them things if I had a chance." "If you wasn't black and if you had some money and if they'd let you go to that aviation school," replies Gus. The youthful Bigger feels the same tightness as Frankie, "like somebody's poking a red-hot iron down my throat.... It's just like living in jail. Half the time I feel like I'm on the outside of the world peeping in."

One might conclude that Wright's novel is a "parable of the essential loneliness of man," but, so far as I know, no one has ventured this interpretation of *Native Son*. Bigger's problem, like Frankie's, is not isolation but exclusion. It is true that Frankie resolves her "sexual ambiguity," as one critic puts it, and takes a "definite step toward assuming her feminine nature" when she finally gives up wanting to be a pilot. The question is why "feminine nature" (or dark skin) precludes being a pilot. Whenever Frankie senses that becoming a woman entails renunciation, she feels the tightness in her chest and rebels.

McCullers endows Mick Kelly with the same desires as Frankie. Mick would also like to fight the Fascists—she imagines dressing as a boy and being accepted in the army. Like Frankie, Mick wants to see the world; she spends her time at the library poring over *National Geographic* magazines. But Mick's first love is music, and above all things she wants to be a composer. It seems initially that she has to give up her goal for purely economic reasons: her parents cannot afford a piano or music lessons, and she must work to help support the family. However, just as Bigger's friend Gus puts race first and money second in listing the obstacles to Bigger's becoming a pilot, McCullers reveals that the primary check to Mick's dream is her gender.

Mick has a friend, Harry Minowitz, whose function in the novel is to serve both as the agent of her sexual initiation and as a contrast to her. Mick and Harry, as a poor girl and a poor boy, resemble Ruth Suckow's Daisy and Gerald with their very different prospects for the future. Although Harry must work to support his widowed mother, he can find a high-paying part-time job; thus he can finish studying mechanics at the local high school. Mick comments:

> "A boy has a better advantage like that than a girl. I mean a boy can usually get some part-time job that don't take him out of school and leaves him time for other things. But the're [sic] not jobs like that for girls. When a girl wants a job she has to quit school and work full-time."

After Harry and Mick have sex, Harry leaves town, either because he feels guilty or because he wants to avoid being "tied down." We are not informed of

Harry's ultimate fate, but he can support himself as a skilled mechanic and has at least escaped the small town to which Mick feels bound. Mick's tiring full-time job at Woolworth's puts an end to her dreams of a musical career. She is cut off from her "inner room," the "good private place where she could go and be by herself and study . . . music," and feels trapped and cheated.

This sense of being trapped is developed in greater detail in *The Member of the Wedding* where the very setting of the novel is designed to reflect Frankie's feelings of being limited and restricted. The Addamses' kitchen, where Frankie spends most of her time, seems to her "sad and ugly" and is most often described by McCullers as "gray." The walls are covered with John Henry's "queer" drawings which no one can decipher. The kitchen is a place where "nothing happens" and, often, nothing even moves. Time passes slowly there (McCullers reinforces this impression by noting frequently that "it was only six" or "only half-past six"), and Frankie, Berenice, and John Henry "say the same things over and over" until the words seem to rhyme. In attempt to classify *Member* as a Gothic novel one critic contends that the Addamses' kitchen parallels the "old dank dungeon" of the classic Gothic romance. Certainly to Frankie it seems a kind of prison.

Frankie cannot find relief beyond the kitchen, for the outside atmosphere is just as stifling. The connotations of hot and cold in Wharton's *Summer* are reversed in *The Member of the Wedding*. In *Member*, as in her other novels, McCullers uses heat to suggest boredom and restriction and cold to suggest liberation. Frankie dreams of snow and ice; Jarvis and Janice blend with her ideals because he was stationed in Alaska and she comes from a town called Winter Hill. But the reality of Frankie's environment is deadening heat. The town turns "black and shrunken under the glare of the sun," and the sidewalks seem to be on fire. The atmosphere is motionless as well as hot. "The world seemed to die each afternoon and nothing moved any longer. At last the summer was like a green sick dream, or like a silent crazy jungle under glass." McCullers's references to heat and stasis create an effect of constriction, almost suffocation, that parallels Frankie's feeling of tightness in her chest. Even the sunlight crosses her backyard "like the bars of a bright, strange jail."

Frankie tries to communicate her feeling of being trapped to Berenice, who expresses it eloquently:

> "We all of us somehow caught. We born this way or that way and
> we don't know why. But we caught anyhow. I born Berenice. You
> born Frankie. John Henry born John Henry. And maybe we wants
> to widen and bust free. But no matter what we do we still caught."

Almost everyone who has written about *Member* notes that Berenice is describing people being "caught" in their own individual identities and being ultimately isolated. It is usually forgotten, however, that Berenice goes on to define a special way of being caught. She says she is caught worse

> "because I'm black. . . . Because I am colored. Everybody is caught one way or another, but they done drawn completely extra bounds around all colored people. They done squeezed us off in one corner by ourself. So we caught that firstway I was telling you, as all human beings is caught. And we caught as colored people also. Sometimes a boy like Honey [Berenice's foster brother] feel like he just can't breathe no more. He feel like he got to break something or break himself. Sometimes it just about more than he can stand. He just feels desperate like."

Frankie's responses to Berenice are significant. To the first statement she says she "doesn't know" but to the second that she knows how Honey feels. "Sometimes I feel like I want to break something, too. I feel like I wish I could just tear down the whole town." In other words, Frankie believes she is caught in a special way other than the first one Berenice explained. Berenice, having accepted the female role, does not mention the "extra bounds" drawn around women, but Frankie feels them keenly.

Honey Brown, who "just can't breathe no more," is Frankie's double in the novel. Frankie feels a kinship with him because she senses that he is in the same divided state that she is. On the one hand, Honey works hard studying music and French; on the other, he "suddenly run[s] hog-wild all over Sugarville and tear[s] around for several days, until his friends bring him home more dead than living." Although he can talk "like a white schoolteacher," he often adopts his expected role with a vengeance, speaking in a "colored jumble" that even his family cannot understand. Honey spends only part of his energy trying to overcome or protesting the limitations placed on him; the rest of the time he accepts society's label of "inferior" and punishes himself.

Frankie exhibits this same psychology. She frequently "hates herself," and her attempts at rebellion against the female role are mainly symbolic. As Simone de Beauvoir puts it, the young girl "is too much divided against herself to join battle with the world; she limits herself to a flight from reality or a symbolic struggle against it." De Beauvoir mentions four common forms of "symbolic struggle": odd eating habits, kleptomania, self-mutilation, and running away from home. While Frankie never carries these behaviors to extremes, she indulges in all four types. She eats "greedily," pilfers from the five-and-ten, hacks at her foot with a knife, and tries to run away. It is characteristic of these acts that, like Honey's rampages, they are ineffective—the young girl is "struggling in her cage rather than trying to get out of it." At the end of the novel we find Honey in an actual prison and Frankie in a jail of her own.

Frankie's principal "flight from reality" is her creation of a fantasy world. The adult Honey laughs at her solution to racism, that he go to Cuba and pass as a Cuban. But Frankie still deals with her feeling of being trapped by escaping to the haven of her dreams where she can fly airplanes and see the whole world. Her favorite pastime with Berenice and John Henry is their game of criticizing God and putting themselves in the position of creator. Frankie agrees with the basic modifications Berenice would make. The world would be "just and reasonable": there would be no separate colored people, no killed Jews, and no hunger. Frankie makes a major addition, however. "She planned it so that people could instantly change back and forth from boys to girls, whichever way they felt like and wanted." This plan provides a neat symbolic solution to Frankie's conflicts.

To many commentators on McCullers's work, however, Frankie's dream is an "abnormal" one; a product of the author's "homosexual sensibility." We saw earlier that Leslie Fiedler initiated discussion of gender in McCullers's fiction when he referred to Frankie and Mick as "boy-girl" characters. This point might have led to recognition of McCullers's portrayal of the conflict between a woman's humanity and her destiny as a woman; but Fiedler went on, in a disapproving tone, to call the "tomboy image" "lesbian" and argue that McCullers is "projecting in her neo-tomboys, ambiguous and epicene, the homosexual's . . . uneasiness before heterosexual passion." Fiedler ends up in the absurd position of contending that Frankie and Berenice are having a "homosexual romance."

Some critics have tried to preserve Fiedler's basic argument by giving Frankie a more appropriate lover. They see her relationship at the end of the novel with her newfound friend, Mary Littlejohn, as "latently homosexual"; Mary's name fits conveniently with this theory—she is a "little John," a "surrogate male lover." Other critics influenced by Fiedler take Frankie's refusal to recognize "the facts of life" as evidence of different sexual "abnormalities." Perhaps she wants to join her brother's wedding so that she can commit incest; perhaps she is really "asexual" (to Ihab Hassan, McCullers's "men-women freaks" are "all bi-sexual, which is to say a-sexual"). The critics who have followed Fiedler's lead leave as many questions unanswered as he does. We never learn what a "homosexual sensibility" might be and how it is "abnormal," what the "tomboy image" has to do with lesbianism, how "bisexual" and "a-sexual" are the same. Because so many terms remain undefined, discussion of sex and gender in McCullers's fiction has been hopelessly confused.

At issue seems to be McCullers's endorsement of androgyny in her fiction. Frankie and Mick are only two among many androgynous characters, including Singer and Biff Brannon in *The Heart Is a Lonely Hunter*, Captain Penderton in *Reflections in a Golden Eye* (1941), and Amelia in *Ballad of the Sad Café* (1943). These characters are McCullers's most sympathetic, and they often seem to speak for her. Biff Brannon, when he sees Mick looking as much like a boy as a girl, thinks to himself:

> And on that subject why was it that the smartest people mostly missed that point? By nature all people are of both sexes. So that marriage and the bed is not all by any means. The proof? Real youth and old age. Because often old men's voices grow high and reedy and they take on a mincing walk. And old women sometimes grow fat and their voices get rough and deep and they grow dark little mustaches. And he even proved it himself—the part of him that sometimes wished he was a mother and that Mick and Baby were his kids.

Biff, who is one of the strongest and most self-sufficient characters in Mc-Cullers's fiction, is shown becoming so after his wife dies. He takes over some of her "feminine" habits, discarding the clearly defined role which had previously confined him. If McCullers implies any solution besides racial equality to the social injustice and personal isolation and despair she portrays in her novels, it is a move toward the loosening of conventional gender roles, toward the more androgynous world Frankie envisions when she wishes people could "change back and forth from boys to girls."

But the critics who discuss McCullers's androgynous characters conclude that "there is something frightening about them." McCullers fails to present women who are happily female and "men who are men (i.e., Gary Cooper)," and Biff Brannon is a "sexual deviate." The next step is devaluation of McCullers's reputation as a writer. Fiedler dismisses her as a "chic" writer supported by New York homosexuals. A. S. Knowles less readily equates androgyny and homosexuality but finds either one "frightening." In his reassessment of McCullers's literary reputation Knowles expresses distaste for the "By nature all people are of both sexes" passage quoted above; he is horrified that McCullers actually "means what she seems to be saying" in this passage. He concludes that McCullers links "sensitivity" with "sexual abnormality" and is thus a less important novelist than she first appeared to be.

Ironically, the recognition of the importance of gender in McCullers's fiction has been no more productive than the ignoring of gender and search for "universal" themes we noted earlier. The main import of the Fiedler approach is a sinister message for potential novelists. If the "universalist" critics imply that novelists should avoid writing about female adolescence because it is not universal enough, the Fiedlerites proclaim loudly, "Do not write about female adolescence if you criticize the current gender system. Those who criticize the gender system are homosexuals, and homosexuals cannot be important novelists."

The universalists have tried to produce comprehensive interpretations of *The*

Member of the Wedding, but to the Fiedlerites a fuller understanding of the novel seems to have been a secondary concern. The readings they have come up with are distorted and partial; we are left to figure out for ourselves why Frankie Addams should be lusting after Berenice or her brother. Frankie's attitude toward sex provides a specific example where both critical approaches have resulted in misreadings. Everyone recognizes that Frankie resists even the knowledge of sexual intercourse. It is not only that she does not understand, or try to understand, such incidents mentioned earlier as her "sin" with Barney MacKean and her glimpse of the boarder "having a fit"; she also conveniently "forgets" both incidents. After Frankie has misinterpreted the purpose of her date with a soldier and has had to fend off his advances, she fleetingly remembers these earlier bits of knowledge. But, significantly, she does not "let these separate glimpses fall together"; she prefers to think of the soldier as an anomaly, a "crazy man."

To the Fiedlerites, as we have seen, Frankie's resistance means that she is a lesbian or a "deviate." To the universalists it is either "pointless" or symbolic of the course of initiation in the modern world—Frankie's failure to gain "insight into sexual experience" shows that initiation no longer entails knowledge and commitment. In fact, there is no evidence in *The Member of the Wedding* that Frankie is homosexual (or heterosexual, bisexual, or asexual). In the play she adapted from the novel McCullers presents Frankie in the last scene swooning over Barney MacKean, the boy she previously hated. In the novel we are given no clue as to what her sexual preference will eventually be. But Frankie does not fail to gain insight into heterosexual experience. Although she manages for a while to keep her "separate glimpses" of sex from falling together, near the end of the novel she gets a sudden flash of understanding. Significantly, her moment of recognition comes after her plan to join the wedding has failed; it is associated with her consequent feelings of helplessness and resignation—she "might as well" ask the soldier to marry her.

Frankie's attitude toward sex is not unusual. The adolescent heroines we have met [throughout *Growing Up Female*], even the sensuous Charity Royall, fear and resist sexual experience; as we will see, resistance to sex is almost universal in novels of female adolescence. The reason is always the same: adolescent heroines view sex as domination by a man (not until very recently are they even aware of the possibility of sex with women). They may, like Mick Kelly, worry about losing their virginity (the woman is traditionally spoken of as "losing" her virginity when she "submits" or "yields" to a man); but they fear most strongly, as Mick does, losing their autonomy.

In his survey of novels of adolescence James Johnson puzzles over Frankie's encounter with the soldier, wondering why her experience lacks the "positive quality" of Stephen Dedalus's sexual initiation. If we look at Stephen's first sexual experience in *A Portrait of the Artist as a Young Man*, we find that his behavior is the opposite of Frankie's. Stephen, hardly the "man's man," Gary Cooper, "suddenly become[s] strong and fearless and sure of himself." Frankie, on the other hand, does not "know how to refuse" the soldier's invitation to his room, she thinks she is unable to leave, and when he grabs her, she feels "paralyzed." In other words, Stephen receives a sudden influx of power, while Frankie feels loss of power.

McCullers treats an adolescent girl's association of sexual intercourse with male domination and loss of personal choice and power in an early short story entitled "Like That." The thirteen-year-old narrator of the story, an early version of Mick and Frankie, bemoans the change that has come over her older sister. Previously she and Sis had had fun together, but one night after a date with her boyfriend, Sis began to act differently. The present Sis has lost weight, cries a lot, and spends her time sitting by herself or writing her boyfriend. The unnamed narrator, whom I will call N., declares, "I wouldn't like any boy in the world as much as she does Tuck. I'd never let any boy or any thing make me act like she does." She thinks of Sis as "dead."

Although N. does not understand the cause of Sis's behavior, she associates the change with her sister's first menstruation which she had "forgotten" for several years because she "hadn't wanted to remember." N. thus connects becoming a woman with giving up of self and being oriented toward and dominated by a man. N. does not want to let "anything really change me," so she either conveniently "forgets" or refuses to listen to information about sex. N. concludes:

> One afternoon the kids all got quiet in the gym basement and then started telling certain things—about being married and all—I got up quick so I wouldn't hear and went up and played basketball. And when some of the kids said they were going to start wearing lipstick and stockings I said I wouldn't for a hundred dollars. You see I'd never be like Sis is now. I wouldn't. Anybody could know that if they knew me. I just wouldn't, that's all. I don't want to grow up— if it's like that.

N. seems more conscious than Frankie of her motives in avoiding discussion of sexual facts and "forgetting" those facts she cannot avoid. McCullers has Frankie express her conflicts in fantasies, as with her dream of a world where people could instantly change sexes. Frankie knows this dream is impossible. She finds society's condemnation of androgyny, which we saw expressed by literary critics, reflected in her own world; after all, one of the freaks at the fair is the Half-Man Half-Woman. Frankie thus projects all her desires and fears into a fantasy that she imagines might be more socially acceptable—she will join her brother and his fiancée and become "a member of the wedding." Those readers who have stressed the theme of spiritual isolation in McCullers's works have noted that joining the wedding would allow Frankie to escape her own separate identity, to become, as Frankie says, a "we" person instead of an "I" person. But paradoxically, Frankie's plan to join the wedding is also a desperate attempt to *preserve* her identity. Her wedding fantasy is a symbolic way of resolving her conflict of wanting to be an adult but not wanting to be a woman, not wanting to "grow up—if it's like that."

Weddings are, traditionally, the destiny of girls, and with marriage a girl officially becomes an adult. But Frankie has changed her female destiny, for this wedding does not entail any of the restrictions that she has perceived in womanhood. Her proposed marriage is not to one man because in her society that implies submission; the marriage is for the same reason sexless. Nor does Frankie attempt to acquire in her brother and sister-in-law a new set of parents, for then she would be a child again. Frankie dreams of being neither a *wife* nor a *child* but an adult *equal*. In reality Frankie is already a member of something—she has "the terrible summer *we* of her and John Henry and Berenice"; but "that was the last *we* in the world she wanted," because a black woman and a child do not raise her status. Her brother Jarvis is a soldier, one of those envied beings who gets to see the world; his fiancée, whom Frankie has met only briefly, at least has the distinction of being "small and pretty." According to Frankie's plan, the three JA's will travel together. She will no longer be trapped in her kitchen but can climb glaciers in Alaska and ride camels in Africa. Frankie will be able to fly planes and win medals, and all three JA's will be equally famous and successful. This fantasy makes Frankie feel "lightness" in place of that old constriction in her chest; it gives her a sense of "power" and "entitlement."

But Frankie's plan to join the wedding is a nonrealistic way of solving her conflict, a "flight from reality" more elaborately imagined than the ones Simone de Beauvoir describes. When Frankie is dragged screaming from the honeymoon car, her dream is crushed. She realizes that "all that came about [at the wedding] occurred in a world beyond her power"; she feels powerless. When she runs away from home after the wedding, Frankie merely goes through the motions of protest and attempted escape. She knows before she reaches the street corner that her father has awakened and will soon be after her. Her plan of hopping a boxcar seems unreal even to her. "It is easy to talk about hopping a freight train, but how did bums and people really do it?" She admits to herself that she is "too scared to go into the world alone."

Frankie now resigns herself—the world seems too "enormous" and "powerful" for her to fight. "Between herself and all the places there was a space like an enormous canyon she could not hope to bridge or cross." When Frankie suddenly puts together the sexual facts she previously refused to connect and thinks she might as well ask the soldier to marry her, we realize that she is giving up her rebellion and submitting to her female fate. At this point the jail image, part of the motif of constriction in the novel, recurs. Frankie wishes the policeman who comes to fetch her would take her to jail, for "it was better to be in a jail where you could bang the walls than in a jail you could not see."

Had McCullers ended *The Member of the Wedding* here, it would have been difficult for anyone to see the novel as "cute" and "sentimental," a *Tom Sawyer* as opposed to McCullers's *Huckleberry Finn, The Heart Is a Lonely Hunter*. However, she includes a few pages showing Frankie several months later. John Henry has died of meningitis, Honey is in jail, Berenice plans to marry T. T., but Frankie is content. She has found a friend and model in the older Mary Littlejohn, a modern good good girl with long blonde hair, pale white complexion, and ladylike habits; Mary encourages Frankie to collect paintings by Michelangelo and read Tennyson. The novel ends as Frankie, with "an instant shock of happiness," hears Mary at the front door.

Twentieth-century novelists rarely leave their characters in a state of euphoria, and those critics who have not thereby consigned *Member* to the rank of sentimental popular novels about adolescence have tended to focus on Frankie's "successful" initiation. That is, the "happy ending" means that Frankie is "accepting reality and responsibility." Louise Gossett contends that McCullers often leaves adults "physically and emotionally ruined" but "brings her adolescents to a healthy measure of maturity." Her adolescents'

> ability to achieve wholeness distinguishes their growth from that of many young people in twentieth century literature about the suffering adolescent. The struggle of the adolescent who appears in the fiction of William Goyen or Truman Capote injures or defeats him with a deadly finality. Mrs. McCullers prefers to educate rather than to destroy her adolescents.

Unlike these other adolescent protagonists, Frankie is not "injured or crippled emotionally" by her experiences.

Indeed, Frankie does not retreat to a fantasy world (Joel Knox of Capote's *Other Voices, Other Rooms*), end up in a mental institution (Holden Caulfield), or commit suicide (Peyton Loftis of Styron's *Lie Down in Darkness*). But the very point of McCullers's epilogue is to show that, while Frankie has "adjusted" to growing up and is undergoing a "normal" adolescence, she has been severely "crippled." Frankie has not merely replaced her old aspirations with new ones just as impossible; she has changed the very nature of her dreams. Frankie's old dreams, of flying planes, of being able to switch genders whenever she wished, of joining the wedding, were protests against the secondary status of women. They were projections of her desire to be an autonomous adult. Now Frankie, or

Frances, as she is finally called, wants to write poetry and travel with Mary Littlejohn. Her new dreams are socially acceptable and easily within her reach. Although she will not climb glaciers and ride camels with Mary Littlejohn, she may tour Europe under the aegis of Mary and her mother. It is permissible for Frankie to go "around the world" but not into it.

Frankie now lives in a permanent "daytime" state, or what Mick Kelly would call the "outside room." To Mick her "outside room" is "school and the family and the things that happened every day" and her "inside room" a "very private place" full of "plans" and "music"—in other words, her inner self. When Mick gives up composing to work at the five-and-ten and stops resisting womanhood to become "ladylike and delicate," she is barred from the inside room: she loses her self. Although we leave Frankie at a younger age, it is clear that she has already sacrificed her "inner room." Her life is "filled with . . . school and Mary Littlejohn" (the outside room), and her summer of plans is almost forgotten. The very kitchen where Frankie thought about "who she was" and resisted "what she was going to be in the world" has been whitewashed.

Immediately after Honey's imprisonment and John Henry's death Frankie would feel a "hush" when she thought of them, and she had nightmares about John Henry. "But the dreams came only once or twice" and "it was seldom now that she felt his presence." Although Berenice appears in the last few pages of the novel, Frankie hardly feels her presence either; she ignores her in anticipation of being with Mary Littlejohn and seems indifferent to Berenice's departure. The fates of Berenice, Honey, and John Henry reflect on Frankie's own situation. The formerly lively Berenice, who once towered over the Addamses' kitchen, is subdued; she sits sad and "idle" in a chair, "her limp arms hanging at her sides." Honey is in prison as the result of drugging himself. John Henry's death seems fitting. Through most of the novel, as Frankie vacillated between childhood and adulthood, she alternately avoided and clung to him. Now, as part of her childhood and her "inner room," he is appropriately dead.

In reporting John Henry's death McCullers juxtaposes accounts of his terrible suffering with descriptions of the "golden" autumn weather—the chilled air and the clear green-blue sky filled with light. The effect is to make Frankie seem a bit callous, for the cool weather reflects her joyous mood; she can hardly feel John Henry's death. Like Edith Wharton's *Summer*, *The Member of the Wedding* portrays an adolescent girl's hot summer, which at the very end of the novel gives way to a chilly autumn. But the passage to autumn has a different import in McCullers's novel. Although Frankie, unlike Charity, loves the cold, there is no glimmer of promise in *Member* because Frankie has not experienced any of the positive growth Charity has. The seasonal motif suggests the possibility of renewal; perhaps "spring will return" for Frankie as well as Charity, but Berenice, Honey, and John Henry are irrevocably lost. At the end of *The Member of the*

Wedding Frankie seems better off than Charity. She is certainly happy, having released the tension of not "belonging"; but the final irony of the novel is that having gained her membership, Frankie has lost her self.

McCullers does not blame Frankie, any more than she does Mick, for this loss of self. As the critical comments stressing her new "maturity" imply, Frankie has done exactly what has been expected of her, what she has been educated to do. In this context Louise Gossett's remarks on her environment seem ironic. Frankie's environment, says Gossett, is less menacing than Holden Caulfield's:

> His displacement is more radical than Frankie's because his society has no place for him, whereas the community of Frankie or of Mick, less large and competitive, defines what is acceptable in the stages through which the girls grow and also superintends their progress.

It is, of course, the problem rather than the solution that Frankie's and Mick's society has a "place" for them and "superintends" them into it. That same society has a place for Honey Brown.

The Member of the Wedding is less a novel of initiation into "acceptance of *human* limits" than a novel of initiation into acceptance of *female* limits. Frankie's desire to be a soldier or a pilot, or Mick's to be an inventor or a composer, could be fulfilled by a boy; these goals are simply defined as unacceptable for girls. Nor is Frankie's ambition to travel and gain experience in the world unattainable for a boy. Gossett's comparison of Frankie with Holden Caulfield has relevance here. Holden's basic conflict resembles Frankie's—he does not want to remain a child but has reservations about the "phoniness" of adults (he projects these doubts into his dream of being "catcher in the rye" and catching children before they fall over the "cliff" into adulthood). But if Holden's "displacement" appears greater than Frankie's, it is merely a measure of his greater freedom. He can at least venture into the world and test it by experience. James Johnson includes Frankie and Holden as examples of modern adolescent characters who flee their homes and undertake journeys. Yet Frankie's hour of running away hardly measures up to Holden's experience or that of Johnson's other examples, Eugene Gant, Nick Adams, or Stephen Dedalus, all inveterate wanderers.

The barriers to Frankie's entering the world are not solely external, any more than they are for Ruth Suckow's adolescent heroines. Frankie and Mick are "protected" (that is, banned) from experience in the way of Suckow's "nice girls," and Mick especially is expected to preserve close ties to the family. But, in large part, the girls fail to journey into the world because of their own passivity. Frankie and Mick, like Marjorie Schoessel, wait for "something to happen" to them—they do not think in terms of making something happen. They dream but seldom act. Even Frankie's desire to be a "member" stresses identification with the world rather than participation in it. When Frankie tries to run away from home, she discovers that she does not have the necessary resources to leave by herself. The details of "hopping a freight," for instance, lie outside the realm of her preparatory experience. She does not have to be prevented from hopping freights; her greatest restriction is that she does not know how or really want to.

Frankie's and Mick's passivity becomes striking when we compare them with the male adolescent protagonist of one of McCullers's early versions of *The Heart Is a Lonely Hunter*. Andrew has the same background as Frankie and Mick; he lives in a small Georgia town with a jeweller father, a sister Sara, a little sister Mick, and a black cook Vitalis. Interestingly, much of this draft deals with Andrew's recollections of his sister Sara's troubled adolescence and her attempts to "try to act like a boy" and run away from home. McCullers had not yet determined her true focus, the adolescent girl, and this early draft is confused because the protagonist, Andrew, is not really the center of interest. We discover enough about him, however, to see how his character and fate differ from that of Sara-Mick-Frankie.

Andrew resembles the female adolescent in being "lonesome" and apprehensive about the future. "He was getting to be a man and he did not know what was going to come. And always he was hungry and always he felt that something was just about to happen." The difference is that Andrew himself causes the event to happen. He takes a walk by Vitalis's house, says he is hungry, follows her into the house, and seduces her. Afterwards, Andrew feels guilty and leaves town permanently for New York City. It seems to him that his experience with Vitalis was "accidental," but it is clear from his seeking her out and claiming to be hungry that he at least unconsciously sought sexual contact. Although Andrew's experience involves some loss of control, as his bodily desires overcome his conscious plans, it contrasts with Mick's and Frankie's in that Andrew acts throughout. It is he who has the desire, seeks out Vitalis, and initiates the sexual encounter. He makes a decision to leave town and then follows through with his decision.

Andrew is an early version of Harry Minowitz, and his two sisters later merge into the figure of Mick Kelly. In *The Heart Is a Lonely Hunter* Harry will be presented as more active than Mick; his situation will also differ from hers in terms of his greater economic opportunity and freedom of movement. Still, Harry ends up a minor character, his function being to highlight the restrictions placed on Mick. Like Ruth Suckow, McCullers includes male adolescents in her fiction but reserves center stage for girls. Not until their last novels, Suckow's *The John Wood Case* (1959) and McCullers's *Clock Without Hands* (1961), do they make a boy the protagonist, and they do not provide him with a female counterpart.

Chronology

1917   Lula Carson Smith is born on February 19 in Columbus, Georgia; first child of Marguerite Waters Smith and her husband, Lamar, a successful jeweler.

1933   Graduates from Columbus High School in June. She writes her first short story, "Sucker."

1934   Travels to New York City, where she enrolls in creative writing courses at Columbia University.

1936   In December, "Wunderkind" is published in *Story*. Seriously ill through the winter, she begins work on "The Mute," which is to become *The Heart Is a Lonely Hunter*.

1937   Carson marries Reeves McCullers, an army corporal and aspiring writer, on September 20. They move to Charlotte, North Carolina, where she writes her novel.

1940–41   *The Heart Is a Lonely Hunter* is published. Carson divorces Reeves and, with *Harper's Bazaar* editor George Davis, rents a brownstone in Brooklyn which develops into an artist's enclave. During the winter of 1940–41 McCullers suffers first stroke. Her mother comes to New York, and after several weeks brings McCullers back to Columbus to recuperate. *Reflections in a Golden Eye* (1941) is published in two installments in *Harper's Bazaar*.

1942   The short story "A Tree, A Rock, A Cloud" is selected immediately after publication for the 1942 edition of the annual *O. Henry Memorial Prize Stories* anthology.

1943   McCullers receives the Guggenheim fiction fellowship. *The Ballad of the Sad Café*, for which she receives a prize from the American Academy of Arts and Letters, appears in *Harper's Bazaar*.

1945   Carson remarries Reeves, who has been discharged from the army for a wrist injury. They move in with Carson's mother in Nyack, New York.

1946   *The Member of the Wedding* is published. McCullers spends the summer on Nantucket Island visiting Tennessee Williams and re-writing *The Member of the Wedding* as a play. In the autumn she travels to Europe with her husband.

1947   Suffers second and third strokes, which leave her permanently partially disabled.

1950   *The Member of the Wedding* opens on Broadway. The play wins numerous awards.

1951   McCullers's collected works are published by Houghton Mifflin as *The Ballad of the Sad Café*. Carson and Reeves buy a house outside Paris.

1953   Reeves commits suicide. Carson returns to the United States to live with her mother.

1955   McCullers spends the spring with Tennessee Williams in Key West, after their joint lecture appearances. In June, her mother dies unexpectedly.

1957   The play *The Square Root of Wonderful* makes an unsuccessful Broadway run.

1958–62   Suffers several severe illnesses.

1961   *Clock Without Hands* is published.

1962   McCullers undergoes surgery for cancer of the right breast.

1964   Publishes collection of children's poems, *Sweet as a Pickle, Clean as a Pig*.

1967   In April McCullers is awarded the Henry Bellamann Award, a one-thousand-dollar grant. On August 15 she suffers a massive cerebral hemorrhage and dies one month later, on September 29.

1971   *The Mortgaged Heart*, a collection of short stories, poems, and essays, is published, edited by McCullers's sister, Margarita G. Smith.

Contributors

HAROLD BLOOM, Sterling Professor of the Humanities at Yale University, is the author of *The Anxiety of Influence, Poetry and Repression*, and many other volumes of literary criticism. His forthcoming study, *Freud: Transference and Authority*, attempts a full-scale reading of all of Freud's major writings. A MacArthur Prize Fellow, he is general editor of five series of literary criticism published by Chelsea House.

MARGUERITE YOUNG is the author of *Miss Macintosh, My Darling*.

TENNESSEE WILLIAMS was one of our most prolific dramatists. His best-known plays include *The Glass Menagerie, A Streetcar Named Desire*, and the Pulitzer Prize-winning *Cat on a Hot Tin Roof*.

GORE VIDAL, novelist, essayist, and scriptwriter, is best-known for *Julian, Burr, 1876*, and the recent *Lincoln*.

OLIVER EVANS is Professor Emeritus of English at California State University, and the author of *The Ballad of Carson McCullers* and *Carson McCullers: Her Life and Work*.

KLAUS LUBBERS teaches English at the Universität Mainz in Germany.

LAWRENCE GRAVER is Kenan Professor of English at Williams College. He is the author of *Carson McCullers, Samuel Beckett*, and *Conrad's Short Fiction*.

RICHARD M. COOK teaches in the English Department at the University of Missouri. He is the author of *Carson McCullers*.

RICHARD GRAY is the author of *The Literature of Memory*.

MARGARET B. McDOWELL is Professor of Rhetoric at the University of Iowa, and a teacher in the Women's Studies Program. She is the author of *Edith Wharton* and *Carson McCullers*.

LOUISE WESTLING is an Instructor of English at the University of Oregon. She has published several articles on Carson McCullers.

MARY ANN DAZEY teaches in the English Department at Mississippi State University.

BARBARA A. WHITE, a graduate student in English at the State University of New York at Buffalo, is the author of *Growing Up Female: Adolescent Girlhood in American Fiction.*

Bibliography

Aldridge, John W. *In Search of Heresy—American Literature in an Age of Conformity.* Port Washington, N.Y.: Kennikat Press, 1967.

Allen, Walter. *The Modern Novel in Britain and the United States.* New York: E. P. Dutton, 1964.

Auchincloss, Louis. "Carson McCullers." In *Pioneers and Caretakers—A Study of 9 American Women Novelists,* 161–69. Minneapolis: University of Minnesota Press, 1965.

Bluefarb, Sam. "Jake Blount: Escape as Dead End." In *The Escape Motif in the American Novel,* 114–32. Columbus: Ohio State University Press, 1972.

Bolsterli, Margaret. " 'Bound' Characters in Porter, Welty, McCullers: The Prerevolutionary Status of Women in American Fiction." *Bucknell Review* 24 (1978): 95–105.

Box, Patricia S. "Androgyny and the Musical Vision: A Study of Two Novels by Carson McCullers." *Southern Quarterly* 16 (January 1978): 117–23.

Brooks, Cleanth, and Robert Penn Warren. "Interpretation [of "A Domestic Dilemma"]." In *Understanding Fiction,* 2d ed., 270–71. New York: Appleton-Century-Crofts, 1959.

Broughton, Panthea Reid. "Rejection of the Feminine in Carson McCullers' *The Ballad of the Sad Café.*" *Twentieth Century Literature* 20 (January 1974): 34–43.

Bryant, Jerry H. *The Open Decision: The Contemporary American Novel and Its Intellectual Background.* New York: Free Press, 1970.

Buchen, Irving. "Carson McCullers: A Case of Convergence." *Bucknell Review* 21 (1973): 15–28.

———. "Divine Collusion: The Art of Carson McCullers." *Dalhousie Review* 54 (1974). 529–31.

Carr, Virginia Spencer. *The Lonely Hunter.* Garden City, N.Y.: Doubleday, 1975

Clark, Charlene. "Selfhood and the Southern Past: A Reading of Carson McCullers' *Clock Without Hands.*" *Southern Literary Messenger* 1 (Spring 1975): 16–23.

Clurman, Harold. *Lies Like Truth.* New York: Macmillan, 1958.

———. "Some Preliminary Notes for *The Member of the Wedding.*" In *Directing the Play—A Sourcebook of Stagecraft,* edited by Toby Cole and Helen Krich Chinoy, 211–319. Indianapolis: Bobbs-Merrill, 1953.

Cook, Richard M. *Carson McCullers.* New York: Frederick Ungar Publishing Co., 1975.

Cook, Sylvia Jenkins. *From Tobacco Road to Route 66 — The Southern Poor White in Fiction*. Chapel Hill: University of North Carolina Press, 1976.

De Beauvoir, Simone. *The Second Sex*. Translated by H. M. Parshley. New York: Alfred A. Knopf, 1953.

Dodd, Wayne D. "The Development of Theme Through Symbol in the Novels of Carson McCullers." *Georgia Review* 17 (Summer 1963): 206–13.

Durham, Frank. "God and No God in *The Heart Is a Lonely Hunter*." *South Atlantic Quarterly* 56 (Autumn 1957): 494–99.

Dusenbury, Winifred L. *The Theme of Loneliness in Modern American Drama*. Gainesville: University of Florida Press, 1960.

Edmonds, Dale. *Carson McCullers*. Southern Writers Series, no. 6. Austin, Tex. Steck-Vaughn, 1969.

———. " 'Correspondence': A 'Forgotten' Carson McCullers Short Story." *Studies in Short Fiction* 9 (Winter 1972): 89–92.

Eisinger, Chester E. *Fiction of the Forties*. Chicago: The University of Chicago Press, 1963.

Emerson, Donald. "The Ambiguities of *Clock Without Hands*." *Wisconsin Studies in Contemporary Literature* 3 (Fall 1962): 15–28.

Evans, Oliver. *The Ballad of Carson McCullers*. New York: Coward-McCann, 1966.

———. "The Case of Carson McCullers." *Georgia Review* 18 (Spring 1964): 40–45.

———. "The Case of the Silent Singer: A Revaluation of *The Heart Is a Lonely Hunter*." *Georgia Review* 19 (Summer 1965): 188–203.

———. "The Theme of Spiritual Isolation in Carson McCullers." In *South: Modern Southern Literature in Its Cultural Setting*, edited by Louis D. Rubin, Jr. and Robert D. Jacobs, 333–48. Garden City, N.Y.: Doubleday Dolphin, 1961.

Felheim, Marvin. "Eudora Welty and Carson McCullers." In *Contemporary American Novelists*, edited by Harry T. Moore, 48–53. Carbondale: Southern Illinois University Press, 1964.

Fiedler, Leslie A. *An End to Innocence — Essays on Culture and Politics*. Boston: Beacon Press, 1952.

———. *Love and Death in the American Novel*. New York: Criterion Books, 1960.

Folk, Barbara Nauer. "The Sad Sweet Music of Carson McCullers." *Georgia Review* 16 (Summer 1962): 202–9.

Gaillard, Dawson F. "The Presence of the Narrator in Carson McCullers' *The Ballad of the Sad Café*." *Mississippi Quarterly* 25 (Fall 1972): 419–28.

Gannon, B. C. "McCullers' *Ballad of the Sad Café*." *The Explicator* 41 (Fall 1982): 59–60.

Ginsberg, Elaine. "The Female Initiation Theme in American Fiction." *Studies in American Fiction* 3 (Spring 1975): 27–37.

Gosset, Louise Y. "Dispossessed Love: Carson McCullers." In *Violence in Recent Southern Literature*, 159–77. Durham, N.C.: Duke University Press, 1965.

Graver, Lawrence. *Carson McCullers*. University of Minnesota Pamphlets on American Writers, no. 84. Minneapolis: University of Minnesota Press, 1969.

Griffith, Albert J. "Carson McCullers' Myth of the Sad Café." *Georgia Review* 21 (Spring 1967): 46–56.

Grinnell, James W. "Delving 'A Domestic Dilemma.' " *Studies in Short Fiction* 9 (Summer 1972): 270–71.

Hamilton, Alice. "Loneliness and Alienation: The Life and Work of Carson McCullers." *Dalhousie Review* 50 (1970): 215–29.

Hart, Jane. "Carson McCullers, Pilgrim of Loneliness." *Georgia Review* 11 (Spring 1957): 53–58.

Hassan, Ihab. "Carson McCullers: The Aesthetics of Love and Pain." In *Radical Innocence: Studies in the Contemporary American Novel*, 205–29. Princeton, N.J.: Princeton University Press, 1961.

———. *Contemporary American Literature—1945–1972: An Introduction*. New York: Frederick Ungar Publishing Co., 1973.

Hoffman, Frederick J. "Eudora Welty and Carson McCullers." In *The Art of Southern Fiction: A Study of Some Modern Novelists*, 51–73. Carbondale: Southern Illinois University Press, 1967.

Kazin, Alfred. *Bright Book of Life: American Novelists and Story-tellers from Hemingway to Mailer*. Boston: Little, Brown, 1973.

———. "We Who Sit in Darkness—The Broadway Audience at the Play." In *The Inmost Leaf*, 127–35. New York: Harcourt, Brace, 1955.

Klein, Marcus. "The Key Is Loneliness." *The Reporter* 34 (June 30, 1966): 43–44.

Knowles, A. S., Jr. "Six Bronze Petals and Two Red: Carson McCullers in the Forties." In *The Forties: Fiction, Poetry, Drama*, edited by Warren French, 87–98. Deland, Fla.: Everett/Edwards, 1969.

Kohler, Dayton. "Carson McCullers: Variations on a Theme." *College English* 13 (October 1951): 1–8.

MacDonald, Edgar E. "The Symbolic Unity of *The Heart Is a Lonely Hunter*." In *A Festschrift for Professor Marguerite Roberts, on the Occasion of Her Retirement from Westhampton College, University of Richmond, Virginia*, edited by Frieda Elaine Penninger, 168–87. Richmond: University of Richmond, 1976.

McDowell, Margaret B. *Carson McCullers*. Boston: Twayne Publishers, Inc., 1980.

McNally, John. "The Introspective Narrator in *The Ballad of the Sad Café*." *South Atlantic Bulletin* 38 (November 1973): 40–44.

McPherson, Hugo. "Carson McCullers: Lonely Huntress." *Tamarack Review* 11 (Spring 1959): 28–40.

Madden, David. "Transfixed among the Self-Inflicted Ruins: Carson McCullers' *The Mortgaged Heart*." *Southern Literary Journal* 5 (1972): 137–62.

Malin, Irving. "The Gothic Family." In *Psychoanalysis and American Fiction*, edited by Irving Malin, 258–62. New York: E. P. Dutton, 1965.

———. *New American Gothic*. Carbondale: Southern Illinois University Press, 1962.

Mathis, Ray. "Reflections in a Golden Eye. Myth Making in American Christianity." *Religion in Life* 39 (1970): 545–58.

Millichap, Joseph R. "Carson McCullers' Literary Ballad." *Georgia Review* 27 (Fall 1973): 329–39.

———. "The Realistic Structure of *The Heart Is a Lonely Hunter*." *Twentieth Century Literature* 17 (1971): 11–71.

Moore, Jack B. "Carson McCullers: The Heart Is a Timeless Hunter." *Twentieth Century Literature* 11 (July 1965): 76–81.

Paden, F. F. "Autistic Gestures in *The Heart Is a Lonely Hunter*." *Modern Fiction Studies* 28 (1982): 453–63.

Perrine, Laurence. "Restoring 'A Domestic Dilemma.' " *Studies in Short Fiction* 11 (Winter 1974): 101–4.

Phillips, Louis. "The Novelist as Playwright: Baldwin, McCullers, and Bellow." In *Modern American Drama: Essays in Criticism*, edited by William E. Taylor, 153–57. Deland, Fla: Everett/Edwards, 1968.

Phillips, Robert. "Dinesen's 'Monkey' and McCullers' *Ballad*: A Study in Literary Affinity." *Studies in Short Fiction* 1 (Spring 1964): 184–90.

———. "Freaking Out: The Short Stories of Carson McCullers." *Southwest Review* 63 (Winter 1978): 65–73.

———. "The Gothic Architecture of *The Member of the Wedding*." *Renascence* 16 (Winter 1964): 59–72.

———. "Painful Love—Carson McCullers' Parable." *Southwest Review* 51 (Winter 1966): 80–86.

Prestley, Delma Eugene. "Carson McCullers and the South." *Georgia Review* 28 (Spring 1974): 19–32.

———. "Carson McCullers' Descent to the Earth." *Descant* 17 (Fall 1972): 54–60.

Rechnitz, Robert M. "The Failure of Love: The Grotesque in Two Novels by Carson McCullers." *Georgia Review* 22 (Winter 1968): 454–63.

Rich, Nancy B. "The 'Ironic Parable of Fascism' in *The Heart Is a Lonely Hunter*." *Southern Literary Journal* 9 (Spring 1977): 108–23.

Robinson, W. R. "The Life of Carson McCullers' Imagination." *Southern Humanities Review* 2 (Summer 1968): 291–302.

Rubin, Louis D., Jr. "Carson McCullers: The Aesthetics of Pain." *Virginia Quarterly Review* 53 (Spring 1977): 265–83.

Schorer, Mark. "Carson McCullers and Truman Capote." In *The World We Imagine: Selected Essays*, 274–96. New York: Farrar, Straus, & Giroux, 1968.

Sherrill, Rowland A. "McCullers' *The Heart Is a Lonely Hunter*: The Missing Ego and the Problem of the Norm." *Kentucky Review* 2 (February 1968): 5–17.

Smith, C. Michael. "Voice in a Fugue: Character and Musical Structure in Carson McCullers' *The Heart Is a Lonely Hunter*." *Modern Fiction Studies* 25 (Summer 1979): 258–63.

Straumann, Heinrich. *American Literature in the Twentieth Century*. 3d ed., 93–7. New York: Harper & Row, 1965.

Symons, Julian. "The Lonely Heart." In *Critical Occasions*, 106–11. London: Hamish Hamilton, 1966.

Taylor, Horace. "*The Heart Is a Lonely Hunter*: A Southern Wasteland." *Studies in American Literature*, edited by Waldo McNeir and Leo B. Levy. Baton Rouge: Louisiana State University Press, 1960.

Thorp, Willard. "Suggs and Sut in Modern Dress: The Latest Chapter in Southern Humor." *Mississippi Quarterly* 13 (Fall 1960): 169–75.

Tinkham, Charles B. "The Members of the Side Show." *Phylon* 18 (Fourth Quarter 1958): 383–90.

Vickery, John B. "Carson McCullers: A Map of Love." *Wisconsin Studies in Contemporary Literature* 1 (Winter 1960): 13–24.

Vickery, Olga W. "Jean Stafford and the Ironic Vision." *South Atlantic Quarterly* 61 (Autumn 1962): 484–91.

Walker, Sue. "The Link in the Chain Called Love: A New Look at Carson McCullers' Novels." *Mark Twain Journal* 18 (Winter 1976): 8–12.

Weales, Gerald. *American Drama Since World War II.* New York: Harcourt, Brace and
    World, 1962.
Westling, Louise. "Carson McCullers' Tomboys." *Southern Humanities Review* 14
    (1980), 339–50.
Wikborg, Eleanor. *Carson McCullers' The Member of the Wedding: Aspects of Structure and Style.* Gothenburg Studies in English, 31. Göteborg, Sweden: Acta Universitatis Gothoburgensis, 1975.
Wright, Richard. "Inner Landscape." *New Republic* 103 (1940): 195.

Acknowledgments

"Metaphysical Fiction" by Marguerite Young from *The Kenyon Review* 9, no. 1 (Winter 1947), © 1947 by Kenyon College. Reprinted by permission of the author and *The Kenyon Review*.

"This Book: *Reflections in a Golden Eye*" (originally entitled "This Book") by Tennessee Williams from *Reflections in a Golden Eye* by Carson McCullers, © 1941 by Carson McCullers. Reprinted by permission of New Directions Publishing Corp.

"Carson McCullers's *Clock Without Hands*" by Gore Vidal from *Rocking the Boat* by Gore Vidal, © 1956–1962 by Gore Vidal. Reprinted by permission of the author and of Little, Brown and Company.

"The Achievement of Carson McCullers" by Oliver Evans from *The English Journal* 51, no. 5 (May 1962), © 1962 by the National Council of Teachers of English. Reprinted by permission.

"The Necessary Order" (originally entitled "The Necessary Order: A Study of Theme and Structure in Carson McCullers's Fiction") by Klaus Lubbers from *Jahrbuch für Amerikastudien* Band 8, © 1963 by Klaus Lubbers. Reprinted by permission of the author and Carl Winter Universitätsverlag.

"Penumbral Insistence: McCullers's Early Novels" (originally entitled "Carson McCullers") by Lawrence Graver from *Seven American Women Writers of the Twentieth Century: An Introduction*, edited by Maureen Howard, © 1963, 1964, 1966, 1968, 1969, 1977 by the University of Minnesota. Reprinted by permission of the University of Minnesota Press.

"*Reflections in a Golden Eye*" by Richard M. Cook from *Carson McCullers* by Richard M. Cook, © 1975 by Frederick Ungar Publishing Co., Inc. Reprinted by permission of the publisher.

"Moods and Absences" (originally entitled "Southern Literature Since World War II") by Richard Gray from *The Literature of Memory: Modern Writers of the American South*, © 1977 by Richard Gray. Reprinted by permission of the author, of The Johns Hopkins University Press, and Edward Arnold Ltd.

"Short Stories and Poems" (originally entitled "Short Stories, Poems, and a Second Play") by Margaret B. McDowell from *Carson McCullers* by Margaret B. Mc-

Dowell, © 1980 by Twayne Publishers, a division of G. K. Hall & Co., Boston. Reprinted by permission of the publisher.

"Carson McCullers's Amazon Nightmare" by Louise Westling from *Modern Fiction Studies* 28, no. 3 (Autumn 1982), © 1982 by Purdue Research Foundation, West Lafayette, IN. Reprinted by permission.

"Two Voices of the Single Narrator in *The Ballad of the Sad Café*" by Mary Ann Dazey from *The Southern Literary Journal* 17, no. 2 (Spring 1985), © 1985 by the Department of English of the University of North Carolina at Chapel Hill. Reprinted by permission of *The Southern Literary Journal*.

"Loss of Self in *The Member of the Wedding*" (originally entitled "Loss of Self in Carson McCullers' *The Member of the Wedding*") by Barbara A. White from *Growing Up Female: Adolescent Girlhood in American Fiction*, © 1985 by Barbara A. White. Reprinted by permission of the author and of Greenwood Press. Quotes from *The Member of the Wedding* are reprinted by permission of Houghton Mifflin Co., Boston.

Index